Fundamentals
of
Bowhunting

Fundamentals
of
Bowhunting

Dwight Schuh

STACKPOLE
BOOKS

Published by
STACKPOLE BOOKS
Cameron and Kelker Streets
P.O. Box 1831
Harrisburg, PA 17105

Cover photo by Dwight Schuh
All photos by the author
Cover design by Caroline Miller

Printed in the United States of America

First Edition

10 9 8 7 6 5 4 3

Library of Congress Cataloging-in-Publication Data

Schuh, Dwight R.
    Fundamentals of bowhunting / by Dwight Schuh.
       p.   cm.
    Includes index.
    ISBN 0-8117-3034-4
    1. Bowhunting.   I. Title.
SK36.S372   1991
799.2'15 — dc20   90-19756
                                                          CIP

This book is dedicated to my daughter,
Margie,
a budding bowhunter.

Contents

Introduction

"I've been a rifle hunter all my life," the man said to me. "But I'm tired of all the people, tired of not seeing any deer. Bowhunting sounds good to me. How do I get started?"

That and similar questions came up over and over as I gave seminars at various sports shops in New York, and I've heard the same thing across the country. Many hunters are attracted to bowhunting, but they don't know how to begin — how to choose a bow, how to shoot, how to get close enough to animals to shoot them with an arrow.

If you, too, want to learn these skills, this book is for you. It's for the person who has hunted with a rifle but wants to try something new. It's also for the person who has never hunted but wants to start now and has decided to use a bow. Its purpose is to help beginning bowhunters build a solid foundation, a base of knowledge, and skill that will lead to years of successful and enjoyable bowhunting. As the title says, it covers the fundamentals, the basics. If that's what you're looking for, read on.

If you're not committed yet, you may ask, Why bowhunting? Probably the most common reason is challenge, a valid reason and one easily proven with hunting statistics. In most cases, rifle-hunting success is much higher than bowhunting success, and the average number of days required to take an animal with a rifle is much lower than with a bow. Hunting with a bow is a challenge. For some species, particularly white-tailed and black-tailed deer that live in dense cover, the difference isn't major, because a rifle doesn't give you a big advantage in those situations. But in more open country, it's a different game. Take my home state of Idaho, for example. In 1988, rifle hunters had a 49-percent success rate on deer and averaged eleven days of hunting for each deer taken. Bowhunters, in contrast, had a 16-percent success rate and averaged forty-six days per deer taken. On elk, the spread was even greater. Rifle hunters had a 19-percent success rate, and averaged thirty-six days per animal taken, whereas bowhunters had an 8-percent success rate and averaged 117 days per animal. Many hunters say rifle hunting has just gotten too easy. They want to put the hunt back into hunting, so they switch to the bow.

It's not only the hunting and the need to get close to animals that make bowhunting a challenge but also the equipment itself. Once you have a rifle sighted in, that's it. Sure, you'll shoot better over the long run if you work with it and practice diligently, but you don't have to. I know many rifle hunters who never touch a gun between seasons, and they do quite well. But with a bow, that approach doesn't work. Shooting a bow is far more physical. You have to pull the bow, hold it on target, and release the string. And, with the bow's rounded trajectory, you must learn to judge range accurately. To develop and maintain acceptable accuracy, you have to work with your tackle constantly to keep it tuned and sighted in, and you have to practice regularly to keep your strength and your eye.

Perhaps a reason for bowhunting more prevalent than challenge is opportunity. Some states have more generous rifle seasons than bow seasons, but that's rare. In most cases, bow seasons are far more liberal. In many midwestern states, bow seasons run three months or longer, compared with gun seasons of ten days or shorter. Hunting with a bow often allows you to take additional deer each year. Some areas around cities such as Kansas City and Los Angeles are open only to bowhunting, and these bow-only zones grow some tremendous bucks.

Bowhunting also opens up opportunity for hunting certain scarce animals. In all states, for example, rifle tags for antelope are limited in number and are issued by drawing. Bow tags for antelope are sold across the counter in several states, however, and even in areas where bow tags are limited, the hunts are often undersubscribed. Some states have special bow seasons for bighorn sheep, mountain goats, and other species in which the drawing odds are fairly good, compared with abysmal drawing odds for rifle seasons.

The timing of bow seasons also increases opportunity. Far more bow seasons take place during the rut, when bucks are more active and less cautious than at any other time of the year, than do rifle seasons. Elk, in particular, have become popular with bowhunters because all western states have bow seasons during the elk rut, and hunting bugling bulls has become a major bowhunting tradition. Many western bow seasons open in August, the ideal time to hunt high-country mule deer, and other seasons are held late, in December or January, when animals are on winter ranges and are easier to hunt than normal.

Montana recently surveyed elk bowhunters, and one of the major reasons they listed for bowhunting was less hunter congestion. Bowhunting is particularly well suited to the person seeking solitude because overall hunter numbers are low. Even in places where there are a lot of archers, bowhunting gives you a sense of aloneness you'll never feel during a rifle season because bowhunting is quiet.

Bowhunting has a rich tradition dating back thousands of years. North America has a particularly strong bowhunting tradition that started with the Indians and continued through early bowhunting pioneers like Maurice and Will Thompson, Ishi, Pope and Young, Howard Hill, Fred Bear, and other great archers. For many bowhunters, this tradition is the major reason for bowhunting. They stress the traditional aspects, such as longbows, wooden arrows, feather fletching, leather quivers, and hunting methods used by old-time archers. Learning the history and traditions of bowhunting can enhance your appreciation of the sport.

You can't see bullets in flight, but you can see arrows, a characteristic of the sport that has an electric appeal for many archers: They just love to watch arrows fly. You can shoot just about anywhere; you don't need a special shooting range out in the country. As long as you're shooting in a safe direction, you won't disturb anyone. You can shoot in your backyard or in a vacant lot, even in your house. I used to live in a house with a roomy basement, and during the winter I set up a target butt down there and shot every day. The distance was less than ten yards, but it was a good place to practice form.

There's also great opportunity to gather and shoot with other bowhunters. Most towns have bowhunting clubs, all of which put on shoots or tournaments of some kind. Animal rounds and 3-D shoots with full-sized, lifelike targets in natural settings, all at unmarked distances, closely simulate hunting. In most parts of the country, you don't have to look far to find 3-D shoots nearly every weekend during the summer, and in winter, you can shoot in leagues. Competing in these friendly contests with family and friends is just plain fun.

Economy is another reason many bowhunters are attracted to the sport. You can buy a good bow, all the needed accessories, and a couple dozen arrows for less than the price of a quality rifle and scope. Treated well, this tackle should last you a lifetime. There are few recurring expenses except arrows, and you can get a lot of mileage out of most arrows if you learn how to maintain them. If you shoot on your own home practice range, you can enjoy hours of shooting absolutely free. Yes, you can spend a lot of money on archery tackle if you insist on having all the latest gear and gadgets. The archery industry, perhaps more than any other, is full of innovators who constantly try to outdo each other with new products. But if you start with good tackle and stick with it, you can bowhunt very economically.

At one time, shooting a bow was a good excuse for not hitting game. When someone asked if you got anything, you could say, "No, but I was hunting with a bow." That's not a valid excuse anymore. With long seasons, generous limits, good season timing, and other advantages, you'll have plenty of chances to take game. And with modern tackle, you can develop accuracy that is more than adequate for hunting. Many hunters bring home deer or elk every year to keep their families supplied with meat, and a look at the record books shows that bowhunters have taken many quality animals.

To join the ranks of these successful individuals, you need the right equipment, lots of practice, and plenty of dedication. Let's get started.

1

Choosing a Bow

Twenty years ago, buying a hunting bow was simple. Your major options were recurve or longbow, and about your only concern was draw weight. If you could pull the bow back, you could shoot it.

In essence, nothing has changed, because bows are still basically mechanical devices to launch arrows, just as they've always been. But in appearance, bows have changed a lot, and buying one these days seems more like buying equipment for a space mission than for hunting. What are all those wheels and cables and gadgets for, anyway? Indeed, space-age technology has crept into archery just as it has into all walks of life. But don't let it confuse you; things aren't nearly as complicated as they seem.

Traditional versus Modern Bows

You might ask whether you should start with a longbow, recurve, or compound bow. A longbow has straight limbs and is generally the slowest and least efficient of the three types. A recurve has limb tips that are curved to give a smoother draw and more arrow speed. A compound bow has eccentric wheels connected by cables to increase efficiency and speed even beyond that of the recurve bow. During the infancy of the compound bow— the late 1960s and early 1970s—most hunters started with recurves or longbows (for simplicity I'll call them stick bows) and "graduated" to compounds, probably because compounds were new and technical, something for experts only. Now the trend has reversed, and today virtually all beginners start with compounds and graduate to recurves or longbows. Since my purpose here is to help you get started in the easiest and most efficient way, I recommend you start with a compound bow. Later, if you crave more challenge or develop an interest in the history of bowhunting, you might want to switch to traditional tackle.

Select a compound bow equipped with sights. Wheels increase energy storage of a bow, yielding more arrow speed for a given peak draw weight. Even more importantly, they reduce holding weight, the weight you hold at full draw, making a bow easier to shoot. With a sixty-pound stick bow, you're holding sixty pounds at full draw, which strains your muscles and limits the amount of time you can hold and aim. In contrast, a sixty-pound compound set for 50 percent letoff hits peak weight at about half draw and then "lets off" until you're holding only thirty pounds at full draw. As a result, you can hold the bow much steadier and take more time to aim carefully. These are the qualities that allow you to learn quickly.

Low holding weight and bow sights go hand in hand. Sights give you a positive aiming point and will help you learn much faster to shoot accurately than you would learn shooting instinctively (without sights). Even Fred Bear, one of the most famous instinctive shooters of all time, recommended sights for beginners.

Dominant Eye

The most fundamental decision in choosing a bow is whether to shoot right- or left-handed. Eye dominance should be the determining factor. A study of world-class archers showed that the top archers aimed with their dominant eyes. If you aim with your weaker eye, you just about have to close your dominant eye, a situation far from ideal. You'll shoot much better with both eyes open.

Normally the dominant eye is on the same side as the dominant hand. That is, most right-handers have dominant right eyes, left-handers, left. But that's not always the case. A right-handed friend of mine couldn't get the knack of aiming, so we checked him for eye dominance and found he had a dominant left eye. He switched to left-handed shooting and everything fell into place. Famous bowhunters Jim Dougherty and Glenn Helgeland shoot left-handed for the same reason.

To check eye dominance, hold your hands at arm's length and cross your hands to form a peephole between your thumbs. With both eyes open, look at a distant object through the peephole. Draw your hands

To determine which is your dominant eye, cross your hands to form a hole between your thumbs, and sight on a distant object with both eyes open. The eye that looks through the hole is your dominant eye.

slowly to your face, keeping the distant object centered in the circle. Your hands will come naturally to your dominant eye, and that's the side you should shoot on.

Draw Length

With a compound bow, draw length is the distance from the string at full draw to the back of the handle (the side farther away from you).* You can roughly gauge draw length in two ways. Using a lightweight bow, place an

*Don't confuse draw length with arrow length. Draw length will vary little regardless of bow style, but arrow length can vary considerably, depending on how your bow is equipped.

arrow on the string and pull the bow to full draw (be sure to use the same anchor point you'll use when shooting). Have someone mark the arrow at the back of the bow handle. The measurement from the string groove on the nock of the arrow to that mark is your draw length. As an alternative, make a fist with your bow hand and hold your arm out as if shooting a bow and have someone measure from your anchor point (most commonly the corner of the mouth) to the outside of your fist. Again, this gives you a rough gauge of draw length. If the distance is thirty inches, for example, you'll need a bow with a thirty-inch draw length.

Keep in mind that this is a rough gauge. With shooting experience, your draw may lengthen an inch or two. On the other hand, you might easily pull thirty inches when standing comfortably at the practice range, but under the variables of hunting—steep angles up or down, fatigue, excitement—you may have to really strain to reach that same draw length. It's easier if your bow's draw length is slightly on the short side.

Draw length will vary, depending on whether you shoot with your fingers or with a release aid. Draw length is an inch or so shorter with most release aids. Variable draw length is a common feature these days, but don't get nervous about it. Start with the measurements suggested earlier and shoot that way until you get some experience. Then you can fine-tune draw length to suit your particular style.

Draw Weight

Draw weight is the amount of force needed to pull a bow to its peak weight. With longbows and recurves, peak draw weight is reached at full draw. With compounds, draw weight peaks at about half-draw and then diminishes, or lets off, to about half the peak weight. For example, with a compound of sixty pounds peak weight, you would hold about thirty pounds at full draw. Average letoff is 50 percent, although some bows have a letoff as high as 65 percent. Draw weight and bow weight are synonymous.

Many hunters shoot bows with draw weights of seventy to eighty pounds, and you might feel you have to keep up. But how much draw weight do you need? Heavy draw weights have some advantages, including trajectory and increased penetration. Draw weight is a major influence on arrow speed—the heavier your bow, the faster the arrows, the flatter the trajectory, and ultimately, the greater your accuracy, especially at unknown distances. Certainly, the faster the arrows of a given weight travel, the more wallop they pack, and on big animals like moose, that is a concern. But any modern bow of sixty pounds or heavier that is well tuned and shooting sharp broadheads will give adequate penetration on animals up to the size of elk, so most hunting doesn't require ultra-heavy bows.

In addition, the law of diminishing returns applies to bow weight at some point, because added draw weight will hurt more than it helps. "Hurt" is the appropriate word in other senses as well, because too much bow weight can cause shoulder injuries, a common problem among archers. It can hurt your accuracy, too. If you have to strain to pull the bow, your tense muscles can cause erratic form, or worse, target panic. Accurate shooting comes from relaxed form.

Bow control is the real key to accuracy and clean kills, and bow control begins with a comfortable draw weight. I'm a fanatic on light-weight bows because I've seen their effectiveness. Tendinitis in my shoulders, caused by pulling heavy bows, has forced me to reduce draw weight to fifty-five to sixty pounds. Many hunters would say that's too light, but I've shot many deer and a dozen elk with bows of that weight and have never had a problem with lack of penetration. Far more important is shot placement — accuracy.

If you can pull eighty pounds with ease, shoot eighty pounds, but if you can't, don't try. Shoot a bow you can pull easily, especially in the beginning. You'll make far faster progress. If your strength is weak to average, buy a bow with a draw weight range of forty-five to sixty pounds (most compounds have a weight range of at least fifteen pounds). If you're fairly strong, buy one in the fifty-five- to seventy-pound range, starting at the light end and working toward your maximum.

To gauge roughly your proper draw weight, hold the bow at arm's length and try to draw it straight back smoothly. If you have to raise the bow above your head and lunge to break it over, it's too heavy. Dave Holt, author of *Balanced Bowhunting,* suggests sitting flat on the ground and drawing the bow. He says it's too heavy if you can't do that. Scott Woodland, an archery shop owner in Los Angeles, says your bow is too heavy if you can't easily shoot fifty to sixty times in practice.

Components of the Compound Bow

Handle and Riser

A bow must fit your hand and feel good to you. Most bows have plastic or wood snap-on grips to fit different hands, and such grips are adequate in most cases. If you want to improve the fit, you can file and sand them down to fit your hand precisely.

These days, about the only reason for using wood is aesthetics, and some wood handles are indeed beautiful. Some hunters say wood is "warmer" than metal, but a wood or plastic grip, or a leather wrapping, will warm up a metal handle. Most handles today are made of magnesium or aluminum, and for good reasons. These metals won't chip and crack

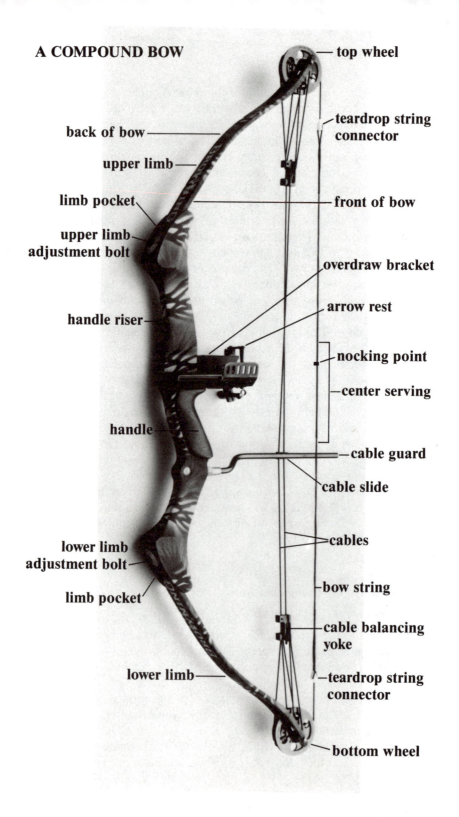

A COMPOUND BOW

top wheel

teardrop string connector

back of bow

upper limb

limb pocket

front of bow

upper limb adjustment bolt

overdraw bracket

arrow rest

handle riser

nocking point

center serving

handle

cable guard

cable slide

cables

lower limb adjustment bolt

bow string

limb pocket

cable balancing yoke

teardrop string connector

lower limb

bottom wheel

nearly as easily as wood, and for a given size they're stronger, which means they can be made slimmer to reduce excessive hand contact and torque.

Perhaps best of all, the structural strength of metal lends itself to the offset, or so-called overdraw, design. Some companies make cutout wood handles, but this feature is far more common in metal. Precision Shooting Equipment (PSE) introduced the first CF (Center-Flite) riser in 1986, and since then, virtually all companies have followed suit. Cutout metal handles work because they give more arrow clearance past the bow handle

Most modern bows have an offset "overdraw" handle like the Broadhead Tunnel handle. This feature assures full broadhead and fletching clearance.

and they ensure complete clearance for the biggest broadheads and plastic fletching. PSE calls its version the CF Handle; Bear, the Broadhead Tunnel; Hoyt, the Radiused Handle; Browning, the Magnesium Overdraw Speedriser; Xi, the Powerflite Riser; and Pearson, the XBC Plus. Whatever the name, cutout metal handles are a must.

Limbs

For simplicity, I'll classify limbs, a bow's flexible power units, into two categories — glass and laminated wood. The glass category includes molded, one-piece limbs made of fiberglass or fiberglass and carbon components, as well as laminated designs. A few years ago, wood limbs were far superior, but they aren't any more. I've interviewed manufacturers, experienced bowhunters, and shop owners who sell more than 500 bows a year, and most agree that glass is the material of choice today. It's not affected by moisture and heat, and it can stand rough treatment. Glass, as a rule, is cheaper, although laminated glass limbs cost as much or more than laminated wood. Arrow speed is a virtual tossup. Wood limbs might be one or two feet per second faster than comparable glass, but that's not enough to worry about.

On the average, wood limbs weigh half a pound less than glass, so most wood-limbed bows are lighter, a nice feature on long treks. That's the only major advantage of wood limbs, however. Don't take this to mean wood limbs are fragile, though, because wood limbs will last a lifetime if given reasonable care. I've shot them for years in temperatures ranging from 100 degrees in summer to zero in December and in rain, snow, and fog. I've never had a problem with them. Bill Krenz, vice president of marketing for Hoyt, said, "Looking at warranty data, we don't see much difference between wood and glass. We get less than 1 percent return on both." If you like a bow in all other respects, don't shun it just because it has wood limbs, but for pure dollar value and work-horse durability, glass limbs get the nod.

At one time, all compound bows had straight limbs. But in the early 1980s, Golden Eagle Archery discovered how to make a recurve limb that wouldn't blow apart, and now virtually every manufacturer offers recurve limbs, both wood and glass. Recurve limbs draw smoothly and look good. But, as most manufacturers will agree, at least privately, they aren't much faster, if any, than straight limbs. The choice between recurve and straight limbs is more a matter of eye appeal than function.

Strings and Cables

Strings and cables connect the wheels on each end of a bow's limbs, serving a similar function to the rope on a block and tackle. In recent years, traditional metal cables and Dacron strings have given way to a material called Fast Flight, which is much stronger than Dacron and stretches less. The result is greater durability and arrow speed. Replacing a Dacron string with Fast Flight increases arrow speed ten to fifteen feet per second.

Initially, Fast Flight strings weren't compatible with compound bows because the strings had so little stretch that they tore the string connectors, or teardrops, off the ends of metal cables. Bow makers have eliminated the problem either by strengthening cables or, more commonly, by attaching the string directly into pegs on the wheels. Some manufacturers use Fast Flight to make both cables and strings; others use metal cables in combination with Fast Flight strings. On the best metal-cable systems, the string and cables all attach directly to the wheels, eliminating teardrops altogether. Most pro-shop owners I've talked with agree that for top arrow speed, durability, quietness, and ease of use, Fast Flight is best.

Wheels and Cams

Eccentric wheels and cams on the ends of compound-bow limbs increase leverage and improve the energy storage capacity of the bow. Round wheels are smooth-drawing, quiet, and dependable, and have a long valley — the point of minimum holding weight — which makes them easy to shoot accurately. For these reasons, they've remained popular among target shooters as well as hunters. But with the trend toward greater arrow speed, round wheels have lost some of their following. This isn't to say all round-wheel bows are slow, however; short ones, especially those equipped with overdraws, can be pretty fast.

Hard cams fall at the opposite end of the spectrum from round wheels. These egg-shaped wheels store far more energy than most round wheels, and the resulting arrow speed flattens trajectory and makes range estimation less critical. That's what makes cam bows popular with hunters and archers who shoot in unmarked-yardage tournaments.

In their infancy, cam bows were known to break, but manufacturers have toned down the cams and strengthened cables and limbs, and now cam bows, as a whole, are dependable. Cams also can be a little more difficult to shoot than other wheel styles. One reason is a short valley, which means any slight variance in draw length alters poundage at full draw and changes point of impact. Jim Pickering, a bow designer for Hoyt USA, said the low brace height also affects accuracy because the longer the string stays in contact with the arrow, the less time the arrow has to swing out and clear the rest.

Half-cams are a compromise between round wheels and full cams: The string lobe of the wheel is round, the cable side egg-shaped. The result

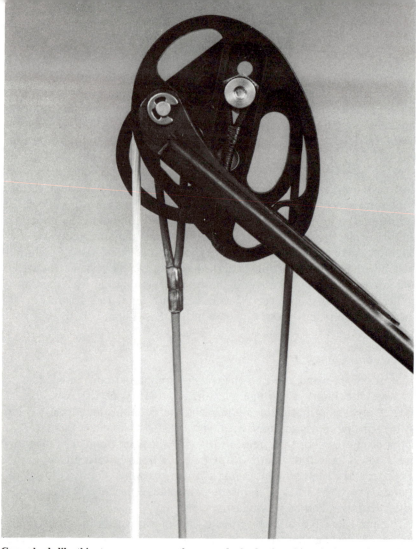

Cam wheels like this store more energy than round wheels. Attaching the bow string and cables directly to the wheels eliminates the need for teardrop connectors.

is a smooth draw and a fairly long valley, close to that of the round wheel, but with slightly increased arrow speed, somewhere between that of round wheels and hard cams. Half-cams include Hoyt's Energy Wheels, PSE's Vector Eccentrics, Browning's Kinetic Cam, Xi's Trihedral Wheel, and Martin's Flite Wheel. For new archers, half-cams are a good starting point because they're reasonably fast but are easy to shoot.

Wheels are made of aluminum alloy on most high-priced bows. On some less-expensive bows, they're made of a molded composite. The composite wheels will perform just as well and they're nearly as durable.

Some bows don't fit into the above categories. One is the Oneida Screaming Eagle, which uses a synchronized cantilever system in place of conventional limb-tip wheels. It looks complicated, but it has proved dependable and efficient. The Oneida is fast, in a class with hard cams, so if pure speed is your desire, this bow is worth a look. The Jennings Unistar is another offshoot of the conventional compound bow, and it also is dependable and smooth-shooting.

Bow Length

As a rule of thumb, the shorter a bow, the faster it is, because short limbs weigh less and recover faster than long limbs. Short bows aren't always faster, but if all other factors are equal—wheel style, limb design, handle shape, and cables—they usually will be, which is probably one reason for the trend toward shorter bows. The other reason is maneuverability.

Back when recurves were king, most bows were sixty inches or longer, but some manufacturers made bows as short as forty-eight inches. My first

The trend these days is toward shorter bows. PSE's Mach-Flite 4 is forty-one inches long. Short bows are handy in brush, and they generally shoot faster than longer bows.

bow was a Browning Nomad recurve that measured fifty-two inches. It looked like a barrel hoop at full draw and increased sharply in draw weight past twenty-eight inches draw length, but it was fast and light, my pride and joy. Among compounds, forty-eight inches is ultra-long. One manufacturer surveyed the market and found that nearly 60 percent of the bows on the market today are forty-three inches or shorter, axle to axle. (An axle is the pin that holds the wheel on the end of a bow limb.)

You could sacrifice some stability with a short bow. Gauging this is subjective at best, but most experts agree that a short bow is more subject to hand torque than a longer bow. Develop good shooting form before you try a bow shorter than forty-three inches.

One other problem with short bows, especially if you have a long draw length, is finger pinch at full draw. High letoff — 60 to 65 percent — reduces that problem, but many short-bow shooters use release aids to eliminate finger pinch altogether. Start with a bow between forty-four and forty-eight inches long. With experience you can step up to a shorter, faster bow.

Adjustable Draw Weight

Variable draw weight is a given these days. Most bows have a weight range of fifteen pounds, say forty-five to sixty, although some, like Browning's, have a twenty-five-pound adjustment range. This is a valuable feature, and the range you pick should depend on your strength and experience.

Letoff

Letoff percentages are estimates at best. For many years, standard letoff was about 50 percent. Thus, if your bow's peak weight was sixty pounds, holding weight would be thirty pounds. The trend has been toward increased letoff, and now many bows are available in 60 to 65 percent letoff. On many bows, you can change letoff weight, say from 50 to 65 percent, either by mounting the wheels in different axle holes, or by changing cam modules. To start with, you might consider a high-letoff bow, 60 to 65 percent, because the low holding weight will allow you to concentrate on shooting basics without straining to hold the bow at full draw.

Letoff probably will not go much beyond 65 percent. The Pope and Young club added a clause to the fair-chase affidavit that says animals shot with bows of greater than 65 percent letoff cannot be entered into the record book. Several states have followed suit by banning bows of greater than 65 percent letoff. The reasoning is that extremely high letoff, say 80 to 90 percent, allows a hunter to draw and hold his bow at full draw almost indefinitely, tantamount to using a mechanical holding device. Most companies probably will hesitate to make higher-letoff bows because of the trend toward such laws.

Adjustable Draw Length

Adjustable draw length is a valuable feature, because, with experience, you may decide to alter your draw length slightly, or you might change shooting style, say from fingers to a mechanical release, which will alter draw length. If you want to sell your bow, you'll have more potential buyers if you can change draw length.

On some bows, you change draw length by changing strings. A longer string gives a longer draw length. On "E" wheel bows, you move the cables from one slot in the wheel to another. Both of these systems alter draw weight (shortening draw length reduces poundage, lengthening increases), so you have to readjust draw weight by turning the limb bolts. With some systems, you can change draw length without affecting draw weight. With Bear's J/B Cam-Wheel and Golden Eagle's Power Wheels, you replace one wheel module with another, a simple process. Browning's Dual Equalizer and other cams and wheels allow draw-length changes just by loosening a screw, rotating a module, and replacing the screw, a neat, quick system.

Overdraws

An overdraw is an arrow rest extension that allows you to shoot arrows shorter than your actual draw length, resulting in faster arrow speed. The overdraw effect can be achieved in many ways, but the simplest and most popular is a bracket from two to six inches long that bolts to any bow. It works particularly well with an offset riser, because the offset assures plenty of broadhead clearance past the riser.

Overdraws can particularly benefit archers with long arms. You're limited in selection of arrow shafts if you have a thirty-two-inch draw length, for example, and want to shoot full-length arrows at a heavy draw weight. But if you put a five-inch overdraw on your bow, you can shoot arrows as short as twenty-seven inches, which allows you to choose from a much greater variety of shaft sizes and weights.

Most pro-shop owners do not equip beginning archers with overdraws, because shooting a fast setup requires some shooting skill and knowledge of tackle. Many of those same shop owners shoot overdraw bows themselves, so they realize the advantage. I've used an overdraw with excellent results, at times shooting with fingers and at times with a release

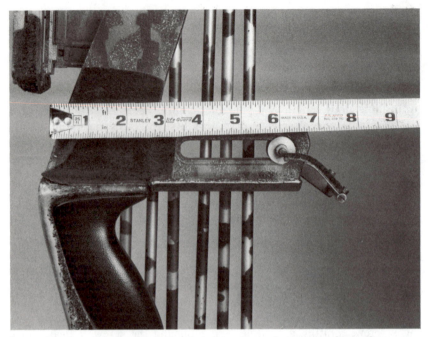

An overdraw is an arrow-rest extension that allows you to shoot arrows shorter than your actual draw length. With an overdraw like this, you can cut your arrows five to six inches shorter than usual.

aid. The main argument against overdraws is their sensitive nature, but I have not found that to be a major obstacle, and many top tournament shooters, particularly those in unmarked-yardage tournaments, shoot with overdraws. Once you've learned the basics of archery, don't be afraid to experiment. You may find an overdraw has some advantages for you.

Price

High-priced bows have all the main features along with frills like a fancy camo finish, a special arrow rest, and metal (rather than composite) wheels. If you can't afford the most expensive models, don't feel deprived. Mid-range bows represent a good dollar value because they have all the important features, they shoot just as well as expensive models, and they're just as durable. Price alone is not a basis for choosing a bow. Its features mean a lot more.

The Perfect Bow

To summarize, let's pull all of these features together. If you've never shot a bow, start shooting on the side of your dominant eye and select a mid-priced bow with the following characteristics: variable draw weight of thirty-five to fifty pounds (for a woman of average build), forty-five to sixty pounds (for a man of average build), or fifty-five to seventy pounds (for a man of strong build); a bow length of forty-four to forty-eight inches; half-cams or moderate cams in the power unit; Fast Flight string; and glass limbs (straight or recurve makes no difference). Start without an overdraw, but buy a bow with an offset handle so you can add an overdraw bracket later as you gain experience. Most major bow companies produce bows that fit that description, and any major-brand bow will perform well for you.

2

Selecting Arrows

The right bow is only half of a good shooting system; the other half is the arrow. Well-made arrows fly straight and hold up under the abuse of hitting targets, animals, and things you don't intend to hit. The variables in arrow construction are nearly endless, and everyone has a pet combination. There is no one best arrow style, but this chapter contains some insights into the variables.

The primary components of an arrow are the shaft—made of wood, aluminum, or carbon—of the appropriate spine (stiffness); the nock, the notched end that holds the arrow onto the string; fletching, the feathers or plastic vanes that guide the arrow in flight; and the head—a field tip for practice, a blunt for small game, or a broadhead for big game.

Shaft Materials

Wood

Cedar arrows have the strongest following among traditionalists, although some compound shooters use wooden arrows for practice and small-game hunting. Some archers say wood is superior to other materials, because it's more forgiving. If that were true, cedar arrows would still have the lion's share of the market, which they don't.

Cedar arrows fly well from any bow. Many bowhunters use them on small game to save money, especially when hunting among rocks.

A major point in favor of cedar arrows is price. If you're not picky about uniformity, you can put together a quiver of wooden arrows for little money. The problem is that wood varies greatly in density, so no two cedar arrows are the same. They can be matched closely for spine and weight, and well matched cedar shafts are very accurate. But matching them takes time, so matched cedars cost nearly as much as other good shafts. Also, wooden arrows break fairly easily, and they can warp and require frequent straightening. The main points in favor of cedar arrows are traditional appeal and good smell.

Aluminum

In 1970, I bought my first Easton aluminum shafts, silver-colored 2018s, to go with my new Wing Thunderbird recurve. Their straight-shooting consistency astounded me. I still have most of those shafts, and they're still functional. Easton aluminum shafts have been the standard for years because of their precision construction, durability, and reasonable price. Now a variety of camouflage patterns add to their appeal.

One drawback is that aluminum arrows bend, and those with extremely thin walls dent and break fairly easily. I don't find this to be a major problem, however. For years I've shot Easton 2213s, which many hunters would consider fragile, and they've held up well. I have shot some of my aluminum practice arrows hundreds of times. They need straightening occasionally, but they've withstood a lot of abuse.

Carbon/graphite

Over the years, fiberglass and graphite arrows have come and gone. Now carbon/graphite (carbon for simplicity) arrows are here to stay. Two companies—AFC and Beman—make carbon arrows. Easton makes

Easton aluminum arrows have been the standard for bowhunting for many years because they are precision-made and durable. They come in many sizes and camouflage patterns.

aluminum-carbon (A/C) combination arrows for target shooting and hunting.

Carbon arrows have appealing qualities. Foremost is stiffness in relation to weight. Even the stiffest carbon arrows are very light, an obvious advantage if you want fast arrows without using an overdraw bow. Even cut full length, carbon arrows are relatively light. Carbon arrows are very durable, and they don't bend. They either remain straight or break. They're not fragile, though. You have to hit something pretty solid to shatter a carbon shaft. Their small diameter reduces their surface area, cutting down on wind resistance. Consequently, carbon arrows penetrate well and drift less in the wind. Special broadheads and matching-weight field points are now made for all carbon arrows.

Price is the major drawback of carbon arrows. Compared with other materials, carbon arrows are expensive, although prices are dropping to competitive levels. Their small diameter can be a disadvantage with certain kinds of arrow rests, because the support arms on the rest must be placed close together to cradle the arrow, which limits fletching clearance. With larger-diameter aluminum arrows, the rest arms can be farther apart for more clearance.

Arrow Spine

For accuracy, arrows must be straight and consistent in weight and spine (stiffness). Wooden shafts are the most variable, and must be hand-sorted to meet these requirements. Aluminum and carbon are very straight and consistent in weight, so the main concern in selecting arrows made with these materials is choosing the right spine.

Spine determines how much an arrow bends as it's shot from a bow. The larger the diameter and thicker the walls of the arrow, the stiffer it is. Spine is further affected by draw length, draw weight, and head weight. In general, the longer your arrows, the heavier your draw weight, and the heavier the heads, the stiffer your arrows must be to fly properly.

Arrows must have the right spine to fly well, especially with broadheads. There's nothing mysterious about choosing shafts if you consult a spine chart. A spine chart is a graph that shows the proper arrow shaft size in relation to bow weight. Spine charts are guidelines based on averages, and your shooting style or setup could call for a deviation from the chart. Before you buy a ten-year supply of arrows, do some shooting to make sure you're satisfied.

Stiffer arrows are more forgiving. On the Easton chart, for example, A is the stiffest arrow in any given category, B is medium, and C is the weakest spine. If you shoot with fingers, pick an A, or at least a B.

Shooting with a release aid, you have more leeway, and you can probably get away with a C. If you are unsure, lean toward the stiff side.

Nocks

Two factors are important when selecting arrow nocks. Nocks should snap onto the string snugly, just tight enough to hold an arrow hanging vertically from the string, but loose enough so the arrow will fall when you thump the string. Shooters who use release aids generally want nocks a little tighter than those who shoot with their fingers. This prevents arrows from falling off the string. The main thing is consistency. All your arrows should fit the string identically, so once you find a brand and size you like, stick with them.

Nock fit is important for good arrow flight. A nock should snap onto the string tightly enough to hold an arrow hanging from the string, but the arrow should fall off when you thump the string. Nock fit should be consistent among all your arrows.

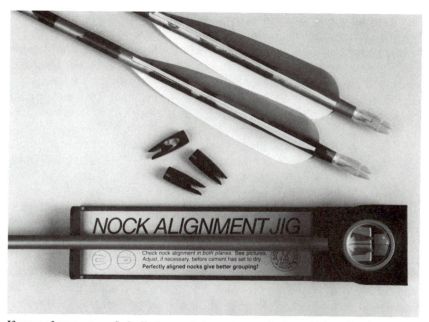

If some of your arrows fly badly for no obvious reasons, check nocks for straightness. A nock-alignment jig simplifies this process. Straight nocks are essential for accuracy.

Nocks must also be straight on the shaft. If a nock is crooked, the arrow is pushed sideways from the instant it is released, and it flies badly. If an arrow consistently flies off target, check nock straightness by holding the arrow loosely and blowing on the fletching to spin the arrow. If you see any wobble in the nock, replace it. If you're buying ready-made arrows from a store, check some of them. If you find crooked nocks, buy your arrows somewhere else. If you make your own arrows, check nocks with a Bjorn Nock Alignment Jig or similar tool as you install them. This simple operation can significantly improve your accuracy.

Fletching

I started with arrows fletched with feathers and shot with them for several years. Then one year, when I was hunting elk in heavy rain, my feathers matted. I met a couple of other hunters who had plastic feathers on their arrows—"vanes" they called them. This new-fangled fletching was unaffected by rain. The archers eagerly demonstrated their accuracy with the vanes.

I wasn't convinced immediately, but I tried vanes and finally switched over completely, mostly for durability. Not only are vanes impervious to weather, but they're virtually indestructible. They will withstand thousands of practice shots, and you can just grab the arrows by the vanes and pull them from a dense target butt. Even smashed in a bow case, good urethane vanes like PSE Pro Fletch will spring back to their original position. (Some cheap vanes won't.) Abuse like that will tear feathers apart.

Another thing I prefer about vanes is their quietness. Feathers rubbed against brush make noise, but vanes are smooth, flexible, and quiet. Durability and silence are the two factors that keep me with vanes.

Some hunters prefer feathers for the same reason they shoot wooden arrows—tradition. They wouldn't dream of defiling cedar shafts with plastic fletching. "Forgiveness" is another common reason for using feathers, and with some setups, it's valid. Shooting off a shelf-type arrow rest, as most traditional archers do, feathers are the only choice, because they compress and slide past the shelf smoothly. Vanes bounce off a shelf rest and send arrows flying every which way. Even with some thick-handled compound bows, feathers are needed for best arrow flight.

Clearance is rarely a problem with today's cutout risers, however. A good arrow rest (discussed in the next chapter) prevents fletching from touching the bow. If you need the forgiveness of feathers to get good arrow flight with modern bows and rests, you need to evaluate your entire bow setup.

Some archers say feathers steer an arrow better. They cause more drag, giving more arrow control. If you shoot oversized broadheads, you may need big feathers to control your arrows. But if you need feathers to control your broadheads, you have a broadhead problem. The market is glutted with precision broadheads that fly well with vanes.

Others say feathers are faster. Initially, they are, because they weigh less. On the average, three five-inch feathers weigh thirty grains less than three five-inch vanes. Assuming each five grains of weight costs you one foot per second (fps) of speed, a feathered arrow identical in all other respects starts out six fps faster. But it doesn't necessarily reach the target faster because, although it starts faster, it also slows down faster. Somewhere between fifteen and twenty-five yards the vaned arrow is traveling as fast as the feathered arrow. It's behind at that point, but somewhere around forty yards it catches up, and the vaned arrow takes the lead from there on.

Here's a summary of fletching choice: For traditional qualities, feathers win. For shooting off a shelf, feathers are the only choice. Speed and accuracy are a toss-up. Vanes win for durability and quietness.

No one can prescribe a perfect ratio between broadhead size and fletching size. A large broadhead acts as a steering rudder on the front of an arrow. Generally, the more a broadhead wants to control an arrow, the more fletching is needed to counteract it. Over the years, three five-inch fletching has been the standard. That's primarily what I've shot, and I've had good results. If you need more fletching than that to control a broadhead, you should try different broadheads. With the trend toward lighter arrows, more hunters are using three four-inch fletching to reduce weight. In most cases, with precision-made broadheads no more than one-and-one-fourth inches wide, that's ample fletching.

Some hunters prefer four vanes or feathers over three because they can nock an arrow either way. I prefer three vanes because it makes the arrow lighter and, because the vanes are farther apart, I get better clearance past the rest.

One purpose of fletching is to cause the arrow to rotate in flight. With no rotation, the arrow would bounce around like a knuckleball. To cause rotation, fletching must be mounted at a slight angle from the long axis of the arrow. Vanes can be twisted either way, right or left. It doesn't matter as long as you're consistent. Some hunters insist on radical helical fletching, that is, fletching that's twisted around the shaft, but again, if you need this, you might have a broadhead problem. Exaggerated helical fletching slows down an arrow unnecessarily and compounds rest-clearance problems. Mild, or natural, helical is adequate. With natural helical, the vane is angled slightly, but its base still lies flat against the shaft.

Heads

Inserts and Adaptors

With aluminum arrows, most hunters use an insert in the front end of the arrow and either a screw-in head or a tapered screw-in adaptor and glue-on heads. Arrow inserts are made of aluminum or carbon. Carbon inserts weigh ten to fifteen grains less than aluminum ones depending on arrow size. Generally, carbon inserts are installed with epoxy, aluminum with hot-melt glue.

Another technique that's gaining popularity is swaged shafts. By specially shaping the end of the shaft rather than using an insert, you can glue broadheads such as Zwickeys directly onto the shaft, thus eliminating the weight of the insert and the adaptor.

For their carbon arrows, Beman and AFC have adaptors that slip over the end of the shaft. These are threaded to accept any standard broadhead or field point. As an alternative, Beman makes field points and broadheads with posts that fit inside shafts as well as collars that slip over

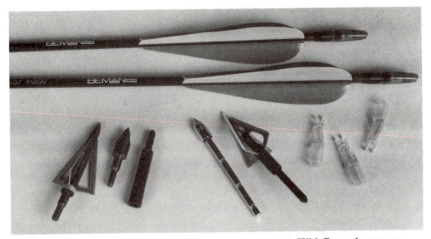

Various point-adaptor systems are available for carbon arrows. With Beman's, you can install a threaded insert (system at left) that accepts any standard screw-in heads, or you can buy special points that insert directly into the shaft (system at right).

shafts. It's a very secure system. By installing these with hot-melt glue, you can easily interchange heads. AFC has a three-blade broadhead that slips over the outside of the shaft, and matching field points.

Practice and Small-Game Heads

For general practice at the target butt, shoot field points. The most common weight is 125 grains, a good all-around choice, but field points come in many different weights from 75 grains up to 180. It's most important to match field points to broadheads. They should all weigh the same so your arrows fly consistently.

For field practice and small-game hunting, rubber blunts work very well. They have broad front surfaces that prevent skipping and deliver good shocking power to small game. I especially like rubber blunts for stump shooting in formal target practice in the field and for shooting grouse. Steel blunts are great for stump shooting, but they're a poor small-game choice because they pass straight through and don't produce enough shock to kill cleanly.

Zwickey Judo Points are excellent field practice heads. They have four spring-loaded arms that catch in grass and twigs to prevent arrows from skipping and sliding. If you use Judo Points with an overdraw, check the arms regularly. After a lot of shooting, the arms can spread and hit the handle of your bow when you shoot.

If you shoot broadheads at turkeys and small game, use some kind of stopper behind the broadhead. The Zwickey Scorpio, for example, which has four springy fingers, slides onto the shaft behind the broadhead. When the arrow hits an animal, the stopper slides down the shaft for good penetration, but the extended fingers on the stopper prevent complete pass-throughs.

Broadheads

The most important quality in a broadhead is accuracy. You can't compensate for poor shot placement with broadhead width, and it's better to give up one-eighth inch in width than two inches in accuracy. Broadheads one-and-one-eighth to one-and-one-fourth inches wide have become most popular because they're wide enough to kill cleanly but narrow enough to fly accurately.

In recent years, three-blade heads have dominated the market because they fly accurately and kill cleanly. Rob Kaufhold, who sells thousands of broadheads through Lancaster Archery Supply in Lancaster, Pennsylvania, said, "Three-blade heads are by far the most popular, because

These heads work well for field practice and small game hunting. Left to right: Standard field point for all-around practice; steel blunt for stump shooting; rubber blunt for field practice and small game hunting; Zwickey Judo for field practice and small game hunting; broadhead backed by Zwickey Scorpio "stopper" for small game and turkeys.

Thunderhead 125, Satellite Titan, and Hoyt Blackhole broadheads all weigh 125 grains. These heads provide good balance and accurate arrow flight when used with relatively light arrows.

they're easier to tune than comparable-size four-blade heads." Bob Kindred, a shop owner in Boise, Idaho, said he sells "about 90 percent three-blade, 10 percent four, a few two." For accuracy and convenience of use, three-blade heads have what bowhunters want.

In the past, most broadheads weighed from 130 to 180 grains, but today a vast majority of broadheads fall in the 100- to 125-grain range, and some hunters go as light as 75 grains. Speed is one reason for that. Reducing arrow weight 5 grains increases speed roughly 1 foot per second, so a 25-grain reduction equals a 5 fps increase in arrow speed. Most hunters will take any speed advantage they can get. A second reason for choosing a lighter broadhead is increased arrow spine. Reducing head weight effectively stiffens arrows, thus opening a number of options for shooting lighter-weight shafts. A third reason is arrow balance. For best performance, a hunting shaft should be balanced correctly. With today's lightweight shafts, heads in the 100- to 125-grain range provide the best overall balance.

To fly straight, a broadhead must *be* straight, so gauge alignment before buying a batch of broadheads. The easiest way to do this is to set a broadhead-equipped arrow on its tip and spin it like a top. If the broadhead (or shaft) is crooked, you'll see a very distinct wobble. Occasionally a head of even the best brands may wobble slightly, so don't be alarmed if every head isn't perfect. But if one brand consistently wobbles, then consider other brands. Ideally, you should see no wobble when you spin an arrow.

Rob Kaufhold said, "Poor alignment is the major problem with broadhead flight. You can tighten a group several inches just by straightening the heads." He uses an arrow straightener by placing the nose cone of the head (just in front of the blades) on one set of rollers, the bending lever just behind the broadhead. The broadhead then can be straightened just as you'd straighten an arrow shaft.

Replaceable blades represent a major development since the old days. If blades get dull, you just replace them rather than re-sharpening them. It's a good feature because sharp broadheads are essential for clean kills, and many people simply won't take time to sharpen conventional heads. Also excellent are stainless steel blades that won't rust. For durability, blades should be at least .020 inch thick. In addition, broadheads should have a positive blade-locking system with a nose cone and collar that hold the blades securely.

Three major tip styles are cutting, pyramid, and cone. Satellite Archery, the largest broadhead maker, has found that the cutting tip penetrates best, the pyramid second, and the cone third (they make all three). Most bowhunters would agree. The pyramid tip has become most popular, however, probably because it's the best compromise. It penetrates well enough, is durable and convenient, and comes in light weights. Cutting-tip heads have lost some ground because many are relatively heavy, but the Satellite Titan, a full-sized, cutting-tip head that weighs 125 grains, has become Satellite's second-biggest seller. Carbon-arrow makers are producing some excellent lightweight cutting-tip heads for their shafts. And Zwickey and similar traditional heads are regaining popularity as hunters replace two-part insert/adaptor systems with one-piece adaptors or swaged arrows to keep weight down.

For all-around hunting, I suggest a head that is one-and-one-eighth to one-and-one-fourth inches wide, weighs 100 to 125 grains, and has three blades that are at least .020 inch thick and a pyramid tip. My personal

Cutting-tip heads like these assure good penetration, an important consideration when using a lightweight bow (sixty pounds or less) on elk or larger animals.

choice is the Thunderhead 125, but several other companies make similar heads. If you're after elk or larger animals and shoot a relatively light bow (sixty pounds or less), consider a cutting-tip head to enhance penetration. I've had good elk-hunting results with Satellite Titans and Zwickey Eskimos while shooting a fifty-five-pound bow. The main disadvantage with these heads is that you have to sharpen them, but that's not a major problem with custom sharpeners like the TruAngle Hone and Bear Archer's Edge available.

I don't recommend broadheads with moving blades that fold into the head during flight and open up on impact. The theory is that they'll fly truer than conventional broadheads because they're shaped like field points during flight and that they'll cut a bigger hole on impact as the blades open. The only catch is that they can malfunction. If chosen carefully, conventional broadheads are more than adequate.

3

Bow Accessories

Certain accessories are required to make a bow functional. Some of the more important are arrow rests, to hold the arrow until you shoot; bow sights and string peeps to aid in aiming; nocksets to hold the arrow in the same place on the string for each shot; and stabilizers to steady your bow during the shot. Never consider these insignificant. Your ultimate accuracy and shooting efficiency depends just as much — or more — on these as on the bow and arrows themselves.

Arrow Rests

A good arrow rest is critical because it's the last point of contact before an arrow leaves the bow. Its most basic function is to hold an arrow in place until you shoot, but it also affects arrow spine and controls clearance. In some cases, an arrow rest even affects arrow speed. These are major variables in good arrow flight, and that's why the rest is so important.

An arrow rest must be dependable, durable, accurate, quiet, reasonably easy to adjust, and easy to use under hunting conditions. It also must ensure good clearance of the arrow past the bow, and it should hold an arrow securely in place.

The most basic shoot-around rest is the bow shelf. The arrow flexes to pass out around the bow.

Shoot-around Rests

A shoot-around rest is one on which the arrow's fletching passes to the side, or around, the rest. Types include bow shelves, solid plastic rests, flipper/plunger setups, spring rests, and launchers.

The Bow Shelf: A bow shelf is a squared off portion of the bow handle, and shooting off the shelf means the arrow lies directly on the shelf, not on a raised rest. Most hunters pad the shelf with mohair, leather, or another quiet material. Not many compound bow shooters shoot off the shelf, but many traditional archers do. This method has some distinct benefits, primarily quickness and dependability. Coated with leather, mohair, or other soft material, the shelf is also quiet.

Despite its good points, shooting off the shelf has limitations. Plastic vanes bounce off and yield terrible arrow flight, so your only fletching choice is feathers. The shelf offers little latitude for perfecting arrow flight. You can change nocking point height, vary arrow spine weight, and alter brace height, the distance from the string to the handle, of your bow, but that's about it. For that reason, matching arrow spine to your bow is more critical than with bows equipped with adjustable rests.

Solid Plastic Rests: Most compound bows come factory-equipped with solid plastic rests. They are simple to use, dependable, and inexpensive, but they leave something to be desired in good arrow flight and accuracy. For best accuracy, a solid rest should be mounted on a movable plate that can be adjusted laterally to achieve proper arrow alignment. But even then, you probably won't get great arrow flight, because the fletching on your arrow will hit the rest, almost like shooting off the shelf. You can minimize that problem by shooting feathers, but you'll have problems with vanes. With many solid rests, contact is so severe you'll see black streaks on the vanes, and I've seen plastic rests that had been nearly cut in two by vane contact. A solid rest can even reduce arrow speed. If you think an arrow rest does nothing but hold an arrow in place, compare the speed of arrows shot off a solid plastic rest with those shot off more efficient rests. I get about three feet-per-second difference between a one-piece plastic rest and a flipper/plunger.

Flipper/Plunger: Flipper/plunger setups consist of a movable arm (the flipper) that supports the arrow, and a pressure button or springy plate (the plunger) at the side. This rest combination yields good arrow flight with both feathers and vanes. Even though fletching may hit the supporting arm, the arm moves easily enough to prevent major arrow wobble. With the flipper/plunger, you can adjust horizontal alignment of the arrow and spring tension in the plunger. These allow you to fine-tune your bow to shoot various combinations of shaft, fletching, and broadhead. The flipper/plunger is especially well-suited to shooting with fingers because the arrow bends out around the rest, virtually eliminating contact. It isn't as good with a release aid because the arrow doesn't flex as much and stays in contact with the rest longer, but many release shooters use flipper-style rests with good results. You can cover the arm with a Teflon sleeve for quietness.

New Archery Products' Flipper II has long been the standard for flipper rests. Other good models are the T-300 and the Super-Flyte from Cavalier Equipment Company and the Arro-Trac from Golden Key-Futura.

Spring Rests: The spring rest or "springy" is a favorite of many hunters. You can move a springy in and out for center-shot adjustment, and you can select different weight springs — fifteen-, twenty-, twenty-five-ounce — to alter flight characteristics of your arrow. To get best arrow clearance, most archers clip the spring end so it's just long enough to hold an arrow with no excess sticking out. You can bend the tip up to hold your arrow securely. To silence the rest, slip Teflon tubing over the end of the spring.

I've never had equally good performance with a springy as with a flipper/plunger, but other hunters swear by the springy. Bill Krenz, a very successful bowhunter, tried numerous arrow rests before settling on a

The flipper/plunger combination is a versatile shoot-around rest. Shown here is the Cavalier Super-Flyte, an excellent choice for archers who shoot with their fingers.

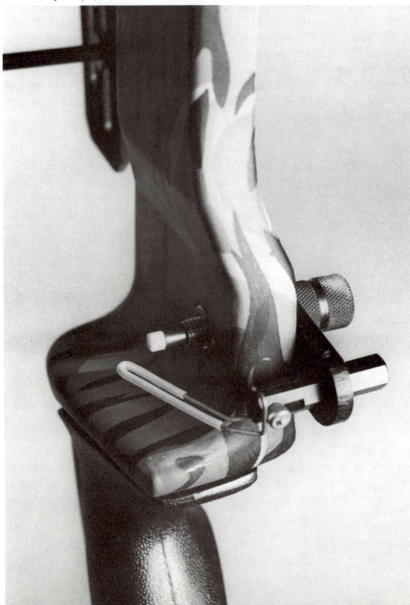

twenty-ounce springy as the best. "I used it with fingers, and now I shoot off the same rest with a release aid," Krenz said. "The only adjustment I've made was to change center-shot slightly."

Launchers: Launchers cradle the arrow, and the fletching passes on each side of the launcher arm. They're widely used by target archers, but they have two major drawbacks for hunting. Most seriously, they don't hold the arrow securely, and the arrow can fall off the launcher if you tip your bow. Also, launchers are more difficult to silence (particularly the metal ones) than other rest styles.

Shoot-through Rests

On shoot-through rests, the arrow is cradled between two arms, or between an arm and a plunger button, and the cock vane or feather passes through the rest (rather than around as it does with a flipper or springy).

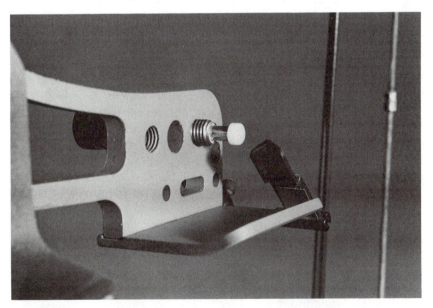

One of the arrow's fletchings must pass between the support arm and the cushion plunger on a shoot-through rest like this one. This is an excellent rest style for use with a release aid.

These rests work best with a release aid, a mechanical device used to pull the bowstring, because the arrow is released nearly straight forward and will pass cleanly through the rest. Shooting with fingers, you force the tail of the arrow to the side when you release, and the fletching generally will hit a shoot-through rest on the way through.

On the plus side, shoot-through rests are fully adjustable for good arrow flight and accuracy, and the good ones are very durable. On the minus side, most are tedious to adjust because you have to deal with both vertical and horizontal adjustments at one time. This means they lack the pleasing simplicity of solid rests or springies. Still, once you get them adjusted, they're reliable and accurate. You do have to take special pains to line your fletching up perfectly to assure a clean pass-through. I've used pass-through rests with excellent results when shooting with a release. The Hunter Supreme, which couples a plastic arm with a cushion plunger, and the Star Hunter, which has two spring-steel arms, both work well. I carpet the arms on the Star Hunter with mohair or moleskin for silence. This may be the best all-around rest because it has no cushion plunger to freeze up in cold weather.

I recommend the following combinations. With a longbow or recurve, shoot off the carpeted shelf. When shooting a compound bow with your fingers, use either a flipper/plunger or a springy. When shooting a compound with a release aid, use a pass-through rest such as the Star Hunter.

Bow Sights

If your goal is to learn quickly, you would do well to shoot with bow sights. Sights simplify the aiming process, allowing you to think less about aiming and concentrate on form. You can also analyze mistakes much more easily with sights than without them.

Sights also help greatly in hunting, because they provide a positive aiming point. That is, in barebow shooting (without sights), you concentrate on a spot on the animal and intuitively line up your arrow to hit the right place, but with sights, you focus your attention on a sight pin and see the animal only secondarily. You don't have to pick a spot on the animal as much as you pick a sight picture. Sights transfer your focus from the animal to the sight, and under the tension of hunting that's a significant difference, particularly in combatting buck fever.

Any sight should be sturdy enough to stand some abuse in the field, and windage (side-to-side) and elevation (up-and-down) adjustments should be easy to make. Pins should lock securely in place so they don't rattle loose once the sight has been set.

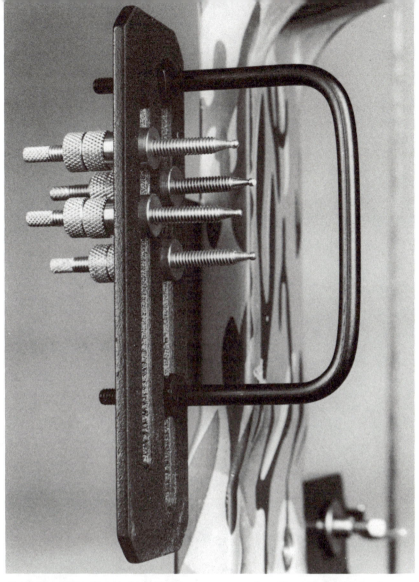

Simple bow sights like this Hoyt Gamegetter are more than adequate. The heads of sight pins should be fairly large for good visibility in the field. A wrap-around pin guard protects the pins, a must feature for hunting.

Pin Sights

Pin sights have small, round balls on the ends of pins that can be screwed in or out for lateral adjustment. Some hunting sights have tiny pins, based on the idea that the finer the pin, the better the accuracy. I think that's a misconception. For one thing, small pins can become invisible in poor light. If you can't see the pin, it won't do you much good in hunting. Bow movement, not poor aiming, is the main cause of inaccuracy, and small pins won't reduce bow movement at all. Tim Strickland, a top-ranked professional archer and successful bowhunter, doesn't like fine pins, so he

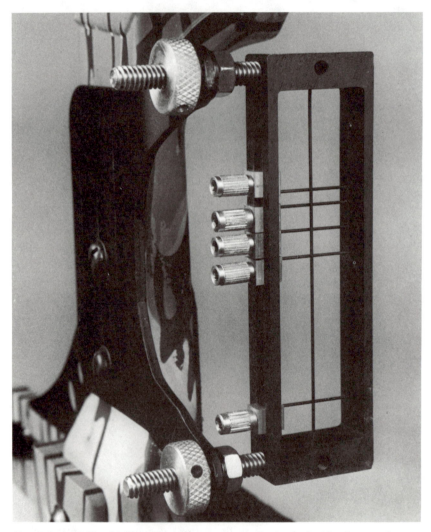

Crosshair sights like this Fine-Line have proven very effective for hunting because the vertical wire assures good alignment on the target.

puts drops of glue on his sight pins to enlarge them to about one-eighth inch in diameter. If you don't want to do that, look for sights with bold pin heads that are easy to see.

If the heads of your sight pins are made of brass, paint them so they will show up better under varied light conditions. Clean them thoroughly with solvent, dip them in white paint, and then paint them various fluorescent coiors so you can see and distinguish them easily. For best visibility in poor light, use fluorescent plastic heads like Saunders T-Dots.

Crosshair Sights

I've shot both pin and crosshair sights extensively and have switched solely to crosshairs because they seem to give a better sight picture. The vertical wire in the sight virtually guarantees correct windage, so your only concern is elevation. Pro-shop owner Scott Woodland says he finds that beginners, especially those who have hunted with rifles, like crosshair sights because the sight picture is much like that of a rifle scope. Some crosshair sights have fluorescent wires that show up well, but some of the best don't. The Fine-Line and PSE, both good sights, have black wires that should be painted as I've described above for pins. The Fisher Crosshair sight has fluorescent plastic crosshairs that show up well in dim light, a good feature for deep-woods hunting.

Some hunters aim with the bow string lined up at the edge of the eye pupil. If you have a solid anchor point, the string should line up exactly the same way every shot. This system works well with pins because the heads of the pins will appear just to the side of the string. But with a crosshair sight, the string parallels the vertical wire on the sight and can cover it if you get the string in front of your pupil. For that reason, I strongly recommend using a peep sight with a crosshair, because it allows you to look through the center of the string.

Peep Sights

A peep sight is a small disc with a hole in the center, much like a tiny donut, that fits into the bow string. It can improve aiming, especially in awkward shooting positions, because it forces you to line up the string with your eye when you otherwise might just draw and fire without good alignment. It serves the same purpose as the rear sight on a rifle.

This isn't to say peep sights are perfect. Once, while hunting deer during a rainstorm, I drew to shoot at a deer and discovered my peep blocked with water. By the time I'd blown the water out, the deer had moved on. Snow and ice can do the same thing.

In low light, you might have trouble seeing through the peep. One evening, as light was beginning to fail, I called in a bull elk. I thought about backing off, but the bull was coming, so I stayed put and when the elk walked within twenty yards, I tried to shoot. But I couldn't see through

The hole in a hunting peep should be large to allow quick aiming and good visibility in low light. This Martin Aluminum Peep has a three-sixteenths-inch hole. Note how this peep is served into the string. With this style of peep, the string must be turned just right for the peep to line up with your eye.

the peep sight clearly, and in my hesitation the bull sensed trouble and split.

Those problems are mostly a function of hole size in the peep. For hunting, the hole should be at least one-eighth inch in diameter, and bigger is better. The Saunders 20-20 and Martin Aluminum Peep both have three-sixteenth-inch holes, big enough to prevent water blockage and low-light problems. You can drill out most peep sights to enlarge the hole. A big hole doesn't hurt accuracy, because your eye automatically centers the sight pin in the peep.

A large hole helps in another way, too. If a peep fails to turn so the hole lines up with your eye, you can't see through the sight to aim. A big hole helps because you can still see through a peep that's a little off line.

Several companies make self-aligning peeps that have a rubber tube connecting the peep to the face of the bow or to the cables. When you draw, the tube pulls the peep straight every time. These rigs work well, although the tubing can break and slap you in the face (or the eye), and the tube can make a slapping noise when you release. Some nock sets have a little blade that slips inside the arrow nock and aligns the peep sight the same way every time.

With free-floating peeps (those with no rubber alignment tube), you must turn the string so the peep naturally lines up with your eye as you draw, and this requires unstringing your bow. To set a peep correctly, shoot a few times to see how the peep lines up. If it's turned to the side, unstring the bow, turn the string a half-turn in the appropriate direction, and re-string the bow and shoot again. Do this until the peep comes back right every time.

To place a peep in the string, divide the strands evenly, half on each side of the peep, and slip the peep into the string. Then slide the peep up or down until it lines up perfectly with your eye at full draw. Make sure you maintain a natural shooting position with your neck and head straight, and move the peep to your eye. If you have to tilt your head forward or back to aim, the peep is in the wrong place. When it's just right, serve, or tie, it into the string so it won't pop out, and you're in business.

An alternative to the peep sight is a kisser button, a small plastic disc served into the bow string. At full draw, this disc touches your lip, and helps you to line the string up identically each shot.

A peep sight won't guarantee success, and it could even cost you a shot once in a while. But bowhunting is a game of percentages, and the odds favor accurate shooting. That's where the peep comes in. It will keep you in line. To simplify things in the beginning, I recommend a self-aligning peep with the rubber tube, but as you gain experience working with tackle, try a free-floating peep.

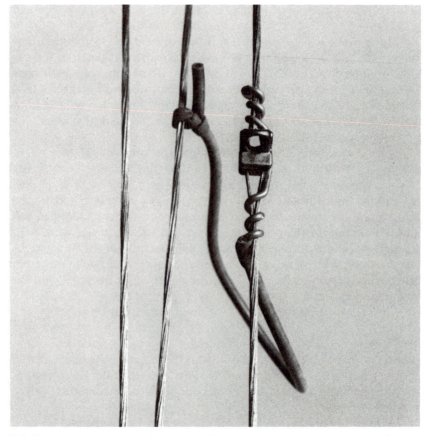

Self-aligning peeps such as the Saunders 20-20 are connected to the cables or face of the bow by rubber tubing. At full draw, the stretched tubing pulls the peep into direct line with your eye.

Setting up Your Sight

You can set the pins on any multi-pin sight for any distances you choose, but the most common setting is four pins spaced at ten-yard intervals, twenty, thirty, forty, and fifty. For strictly close-range shooting at known distances, say for hunting from a tree stand or turkey hunting, you might find a single sight pin set at fifteen or twenty yards simpler to use. Some hunters use two pins set for something like twenty and fifty yards, and they compensate for various yardages by holding over or under. That is, for a thirty-yard shot, they aim with the twenty-yard pin by holding it over the target, and for a forty-yard shot, they aim by holding the fifty-yard pin under the target. You can arrange sight pins any way that works for you, but I recommend ten-yard increments from twenty to fifty yards for beginners.

Let's assume you've chosen that arrangement. To sight-in your bow, set the close-range sight first. Stand exactly twenty yards from your target and, aiming with the top pin, shoot a couple of arrows to give yourself a starting point. To bring your arrows on target (assuming they were off), move the sight pins to the point of impact. That is, if the arrows hit high, move the sight pin up, if low, move it down. If the arrows hit right, move the sight to the right, if left, then left. Continue to shoot and move the sight pin until you consistently hit where you aim.

Now line up all your pins vertically. You can use your bow string as a straight edge and align the pins with it. Your sight pins must be in a straight vertical line (with a crosshair, the vertical wire must parallel the bow string). This all assumes you hold your bow vertically when you shoot — which you should. Now measure off exactly fifty yards, and sight in your fifty-yard pin using the same procedure as for twenty. With these two pins set, you can pretty well fill in the gaps for thirty and forty yards. The pins should progressively get farther apart.

Nocksets

For consistency, your arrow must be nocked in exactly the same place every shot. That's where the nockset comes in. Nocksets clamp onto the string to act as a stopper so the arrow can't slide up the string. They come in many forms, but the simplest are little rubber-lined metal clamps. These are easy to install, and with special pliers, they can be loosened and moved up and down the string for fine tuning. The best I've found are made by Saunders.

Stabilizers

A stabilizer is a metal rod that screws into the riser of the bow. One function is to reduce torque, or twisting. A stabilizer adds weight and serves as a counterbalance, preventing the bow from jumping when the arrow is released. The longer the stabilizer, the better it works. That's the primary purpose of long stabilizers on target bows. Those aren't practical for hunting, but a short stabilizer does the same thing to a lesser degree.

Another purpose of a stabilizer is to add weight, so you can hold steadier at full draw. That's particularly helpful in the wind, or when you're tired and shaky and the bow tends to bounce around. Added weight helps to smooth out shooting errors.

A stabilizer helps to silence and stabilize a bow. It's especially helpful on short, lightweight bows. The Saunders Torque Tamer shown here has rubber bushings to absorb vibration.

A stabilizer also improves the balance of a bow and reduces vibration and noise. No bow is 100-percent efficient. Only a certain percent (70 to 80 on the average) of the bow's energy is imparted to the arrow, and the rest of the energy vibrates through the bow. The more energy your bow stores and the lighter your arrows, the worse this problem becomes. A heavy stabilizer absorbs some of that excess energy and helps to quiet the bow.

If your bow is excessively short or lightweight, then a stabilizer can help you. But most compound bows equipped with quivers full of arrows weigh at least five pounds, some six and more. With that much weight, they're already fairly stable, and a stabilizer is only an added burden. With experience, you can decide for yourself whether a stabilizer enhances your shooting enough to make it worth the weight. But for starting out, a stabilizer usually is unnecessary.

Wrist Sling

For accurate shooting, your bow hand must be relaxed throughout the shot. The only problem is that you could drop the bow after you've released. That's a particular problem when learning to shoot with a release aid. The device can go off unexpectedly, and you very likely will drop your bow.

A wrist sling — a strap that attaches to the bow handle and loops around your wrist — can prevent that. The sling should remain loose, not binding your hand as you shoot. You may choose not to use a wrist sling for hunting, but it can be a useful accessory for learning to shoot.

4

Shooting Aids

The previous chapter covered accessories that attach to the bow. This chapter deals with aids to help you perfect your shooting and hunting. These include shooting gloves and finger tabs to protect your fingers (if you release the string with your fingers); release aids, mechanical devices used to draw and release the bow string; arm guards and chest protectors to prevent the bow string from hitting your arm or chest; quivers to hold arrows while you're hunting; and rangefinders to help you accurately judge shooting distance.

Finger Shooting

Shooting Gloves

At one time, most archers used leather shooting gloves, which have individual finger stalls. A shooting glove is durable and is always in place, ready for action, so it's fast and convenient. Many traditional archers still favor shooting gloves because of the traditional flavor and the speed of nocking and shooting an arrow.

Shooting gloves aren't as widely used now as they once were, however, for several reasons. The stalls are made of a single layer of leather, which doesn't provide much padding, so your fingers can get sore with a lot of shooting. After long use, the stalls tend to groove and the string can't slip

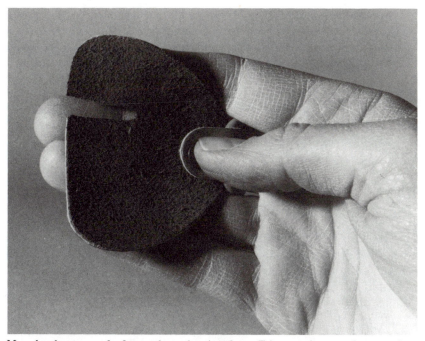

Many bowhunters prefer finger tabs to shooting gloves. Tabs come in many shapes, styles, and materials. This leather tab is made by Golden Key-Futura.

away smoothly. And, because your fingers operate independently of each other, you have a lot more potential for a rough release than you do with other finger protectors.

One other drawback is that your fingers sweat inside the stalls, which makes the leather soggy and slippery. I've had the string pull a sweaty glove right off my fingers. A shooting glove may satisfy traditional longings, and it may allow the fastest reaction, but other forms of finger protection are better suited for hunting.

Finger Tabs

Most finger tabs, a section of leather or plastic to protect the shooting fingers, are held in place by rings of plastic, rubber, or leather around the middle finger. With a tab, your fingers can breathe, which eliminates the sweat problem. You can rotate a tab to the back of your hand, out of the way for working with your hands. Also, in cold weather you can slip a tab over wool gloves and shoot with no major adjustments. With a shooting glove, you have to cut the fingers out of gloves.

Tabs are made from a variety of materials. Hair tabs are slick and give a good release, but once the hair wears off, you end up with rough, bare leather. That's why I prefer smooth leather tabs. They're slick enough to work well and don't change consistency. Plastic tabs are also good. The Saunders Fab Tab, for example, consists of a felt pad sandwiched between two layers of slick plastic. It's comfortable to shoot, and wet weather doesn't affect the plastic.

One good feature on any tab is a finger spacer that prevents pinching the arrow between your fingers. Some hunters pinch the nock so hard at full draw they put a noticeable bend in the arrow, which causes poor arrow flight. A finger spacer reduces pinching and assures a smooth release and good arrow flight.

Shooting with fingers causes an arrow to bend radically upon release of the bow string (most hunters call this paradox). For that reason, shoot-through rests are not ideal for archers who shoot with their fingers. As discussed in chapter 3, better rests with fingers are shoot-around rests, such as the flipper/plunger or springy.

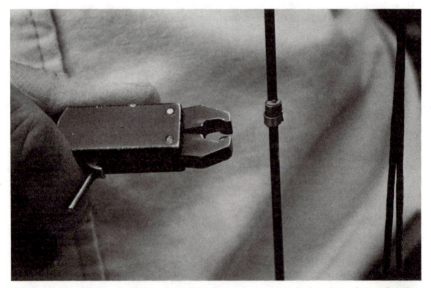

This Scott release has caliper-style jaws that close when you push the trigger forward and open when you pull the trigger. A mechanical release grips the string at only one point, making it potentially more accurate than fingers. Notice the double nockset on this string to prevent slippage.

Shooting with fingers is simple and reliable. You can feel the string and nock, and you can shoot an arrow quickly. Most release-aid shooters have blown opportunities because they fumbled with their release, but that's rare with fingers. Conceivably, you could lose your finger tab or glove, but that's not likely, since it's attached to your hand. Besides, you should always have a spare or two with you, and even if you don't, you can shoot with your bare fingers in a bind.

I recommend starting with a smooth leather or plastic finger tab with a finger spacer. You can move on from there to try other methods.

Mechanical Release Aids

For seventeen years, I shot with fingers and shot very well. But in the interest of learning about all aspects of archery, I decided to try a release and now have shot and hunted with one extensively. A release aid offers the greatest potential shooting accuracy, a fact that is evident in target archery. Release shooters are placed in a class by themselves because, as a whole, they're more accurate than fingers shooters.

Closely related to accuracy is consistency. In shooting with fingers, you grip the string across a broad area, and you have three contact points (two if you draw with two fingers). All that contact makes it hard to let go of the string identically every time. A release aid, in contrast, grips the string at one tiny point, so the string slips away smoothly, shot after shot, with little variation.

A third benefit is the surprise element. Ideally, you should be totally surprised any time you let go of the bow string. But with fingers, it's hard to do that. At some point, your mind says, "Now is the time. Open your fingers and let go." The result can be a rough release. On the other hand, if you squeeze the trigger on a release aid slowly, you'll truly be surprised when the bow goes off. This feature can be especially beneficial if you suffer from target panic or "freezing." The surprise element has helped many archers overcome target panic.

Under ideal conditions—at the target butt on a calm day—the gain in accuracy and consistency achieved with release aids may seem insignificant, but it can be important when your hands are half frozen, or after you've hiked all day and are numb with fatigue. Your fingers may let you down, but a release won't. That's not to say a release aid will make you instantly perfect. It takes practice, just like any other shooting method. The specifics of using a release aid are discussed in chapter 5, "Learning to Shoot."

There are three basic styles of release aids: finger-held, concho, and wrist-strap. I'm notorious for losing things, so I use a wrist-strap model.

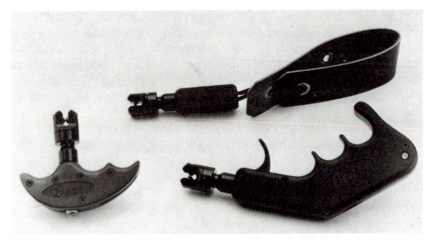

The three basic styles of release aids are the finger-held, the concho, and the wrist strap.

During a hunt, the release is buckled around my wrist, and during off hours, it's strapped to my bow. The one problem with a wrist model is that you have to attach it to the string when you're ready to shoot, so you could fumble at the moment of truth. Many hand-held and concho models can be clipped onto the string ahead of the shot, but you can misplace a hand-held model or leave it lying at your last rest break, two miles away.

With a wrist-strap model, all the pressure is on your wrist, leaving your fingers relaxed. With a finger model, all the tension is on your fingers. With a concho, you grip a center tube, and then most of the pressure is applied with the side of your hand against a plate. I like the wrist strap, but you might find you prefer one of the others.

Release aids attach to the string in various ways, but the main two are with a rope or metal jaws. Rope releases are accurate and gentle on bow strings, but they can be slow to use. Some hunters use rope releases, but these devices are better suited for target archery.

The variations in metal-jaw releases are endless. My favorite, made by Scott, has caliper-style jaws. It lets the string go straight forward, rather than sliding to the side as pin-type jaws do. The caliper jaws are easy on strings. One criticism of release aids is excessive string wear, but I've never had a problem with that. If a release aid does damage a string, check the jaws of the release for burrs. Those can eat servings in a hurry. Smooth out the burrs with fine emery cloth.

Unlike fingers, a release exerts all its pressure upward against a nocked arrow, so you must reinforce your nocking point to keep it from sliding up. Some archers wrap dental floss or serving string above the nocking point. I just clamp two nocksets together, one above the other, and I've never had a nocking point move.

Some archers put a rubber O-ring on the string below the arrow nock as a cushion between the release and the arrow. Some who want to clip a hand-held release on the string place a second nockset below the release to keep it from sliding down the string. These setups are okay, but I don't use them because there's always a potential, in the heat of action, for nocking your arrow below an O-ring or the lower nocking point. Needless to say, your arrow won't go where you aim. For best results, keep your string setup simple.

Release aids let the string go straight forward, so the arrow bends little when shot. The best arrow rest style for use with a release is the shoot-through rest (see "Arrow Rests" in chapter 3).

A release may be slower than fingers, but with practice you can be fast enough for hunting. Proper care can prevent most malfunctions. On my first hunt with a release, I fell down a dirt bank and crammed the release full of dirt. I've also had release aids rust up in wet weather. Simple precautions will prevent such problems. In dry weather, wash the release thoroughly with solvent to eliminate all dust-catching oil. In wet weather, oil your release to keep it from rusting. Most important, always carry a spare. That's the only absolute guarantee against loss and malfunction.

A release won't make you a better hunter, but it can promote consistency under field conditions, which means more clean kills.

Arm Guards and Chest Protectors

An arm guard might seem insignificant, but it can play a big part in hunting success. At the very least, it can save you some pain. When starting out, you'll probably hit the inside of your bow arm with the string when you release, which will cause painful bruises. To prevent that, wear a large arm guard that covers the entire inside of your arm.

With experience, you'll learn to shoot so the string doesn't hit your arm, so after a while the arm guard really won't be needed to protect your arm. But that doesn't mean it's no longer valuable.

I vividly recall watching a big mule deer walking slowly my way. I was sitting on a rim, ready and waiting, anticipating my elation over taking such a fine buck. I drew my bow well before the buck arrived, and when he stopped broadside at twenty-five yards, I aimed carefully and released. The arrow fluttered from my bow and crashed to the ground halfway to the deer. As the deer raced away, I saw the reason for my miss. Earlier, a cold wind had come up, and I'd slipped on a wool shirt. I'd forgotten to put my arm guard over the shirt, and the baggy sleeve had snagged my bow string.

That's the reason for wearing an arm guard. It doesn't have to be anything fancy, just something to hold your sleeve out of the way of your bow string. A chest protector performs a similar function. Normally it's not needed, but if you're wearing bulky or baggy clothing, as you might in cold weather, a chest protector can be valuable in holding your clothes out of the way.

Quivers

The primary function of a quiver is to protect your arrows and store them where you can reach they easily. All quivers have a hood to hold and protect broadheads and a series of arrow grippers to hold the shafts securely. There are three basic types of quivers — bow, hip, and back.

Bow Quivers

By far the most popular type is the bow quiver, probably because of convenience. As the name suggests, a bow quiver attaches to your bow, making your bow and arrows one handy unit. A bow quiver offers a couple of other advantages. Many hunters put stabilizers on their bows to add weight and reduce torque. A quiver may not be as efficient, but it

The bow quiver has been first choice among bowhunters since the 1950s because it is convenient and makes the bow and arrows one handy unit.

accomplishes the same purpose by adding weight that stabilizes the bow. And as long as it's solidly attached to the bow it also absorbs excess energy and vibration to help silence the bow.

One drawback of the bow quiver is that it sits on the side of the bow, thus throwing the bow slightly off balance. Some archers say that affects accuracy, but I think the difference is insignificant. Also, some archers don't like bow quivers because they can make a bow uncomfortably heavy to carry. But most of us who favor bow quivers feel the convenience is worth the sacrifice.

To minimize a bow quiver's effect on accuracy, don't tune and sight-in your bow with a quiver attached, then take it off for hunting. Either shoot the bow with the quiver attached all the time or not at all.

When buying a quiver, think safety. The broadhead hood should be deep enough to completely cover the broadheads. No part of the blades should show. The rubber in the hood should be solid enough to hold the heads securely, and the shaft grippers must hold the arrows tightly, so they can't get yanked out as you're going through brush. If you shoot small-diameter shafts, particularly carbon shafts, buy a quiver with small grippers made especially for these arrows. Companies like Sagittarius make quivers especially for carbon shafts.

A quiver also must be strong and silent. Some one-piece plastic quivers are made for convenience, with quick-detach systems. This style is okay if you use a quiver just to carry your arrows to a stand, and then remove the quiver for shooting. Otherwise, I don't recommend it. The quivers pop when you shoot, and they don't hold the arrows securely.

The best quivers bolt directly to the bow at two points. The two-piece Sagittarius Pegasus and a similar model made by Hoyt slip under the limb bolts. This is the most solid system because it can't loosen and rattle unless your bow limbs are ready to fall off. Other styles screw directly to the side of the bow, either with dovetail brackets or with screws directly into the riser. Make sure the quiver you select is compatible with sights and other components. You're probably best off buying a complete system from one company, like PSE's channeled system or Browning's Twist-Lock Quiver made specifically for its bows.

Most bow quivers hold eight arrows, and I think that's about right. In my quiver, I carry six broadheads and two blunts for practice and grouse shooting.

Hip Quivers

For the reasons pointed out above—poor bow balance and excessive weight—some hunters don't like bow quivers. At one time, the hip or belt quiver was fairly popular, but it was overshadowed for many years by the

The Adams Hip Holster, an indestructible cowhide unit with reliable hood and arrow grippers, is perhaps the best hip quiver on the market. Notice that the broadheads are totally buried in foam, a must for safety with any quiver.

Back quivers come in many different styles. The Catquiver IV shown here not only carries a good supply of arrows but can handle enough gear for overnight outings.

bow quiver. In recent years, however, the hip quiver has regained popularity. This is due largely to Chuck Adams, a stickler on bow tuning and accuracy who favors and promotes the hip quiver. His own brand, the Adams Arrow Holster, is made of heavy leather with an excellent broadhead hood and shaft grippers. It's the best I've seen. Several other companies market similar quivers, some coated with PolarFleece for camouflage and silence.

Back Quivers

In the days when the longbow was king, open back quivers were the obvious choice. They held lots of arrows and enabled the archer to grab one arrow after another and shoot them in rapid succession. But these quivers hold the arrows loosely, so they can rattle and even fall out, a major safety hazard. Shoulder quivers are okay for storing a batch of practice arrows, but they're not the best choice for hunting. Their main appeal is tradition.

Some modern back quivers, in contrast, are great for hunting. Most of these have foam-padded plates at each end. The broadheads are stuck into one plate and the nocks into the other, a system that holds the arrows securely. The one drawback is that all the arrows must be the same length. This can be a problem, since practice arrows with blunts may be shorter than broadhead arrows.

Back quivers protect fletching from the elements, a good feature if you're using feather fletching in wet weather. The back quiver holds the arrows in the middle of your back, where they're out of the way for hiking and crawling through brush. Many modern back quivers, such as Cat Quivers made by Rancho Safari, have built-in packs, so the quiver doubles as a hunting pack. If you decide you don't like bow quivers, a good back quiver is worth considering.

Rangefinders

With all the emphasis on speed these days, you might think arrow trajectory is no longer a problem. That isn't true. For even the fastest bows, projectile drop is greater at 30 yards than it is at 300 yards for the average rifle. That's why inaccurate range estimation is the major reason for missed shots.

A good optical rangefinder can add to your hunting success. The Ranging 80/2 is accurate to at least fifty yards.

That's where the rangefinder comes in. If you shoot instinctively, of course, a rangefinder can't help you, because you make no attempt to estimate range. But with sights, accurate range estimation is essential to accuracy. With practice, you can develop a good eye for estimating range, but that system is still fallible. A rangefinder can improve your accuracy, especially at distances beyond 30 yards.

There are two basic types of rangefinder—stadia and optical. With stadia rangefinders, you estimate range by comparing a calibrated scale to your target. Many stadia rangefinders are bow mounted, often as part of the sight. This system is fast, but it has shortcomings. First, it assumes all animals of a given species are the same size, which isn't true. It also assumes you'll have a good broadside view of the animal, which may not happen.

Optical rangefinders (also called coincidence rangefinders) operate on the principle of triangulation. They have two windows, and a combination of lenses and prisms inside produces two images of the object you're viewing. As you look through the viewfinder, you turn a dial until the images coincide (thus the name coincidence). Then you read the distance off the dial. These can be very accurate out to 50 yards or farther. The Ranging 80/2 and TLR 75 are practical bowhunting rangefinders. They're most useful for measuring distances from a tree stand to surrounding objects, so you know various ranges before a deer comes on the scene. They're also excellent in stalking situations, when you have time to take a reading off a deer's antlers.

5

Learning to Shoot

Taking animals with a bow requires two accomplishments—getting close and making the shot. Most bowhunters and writers stress the first part—after all, archery is a close-range sport—but putting the arrow in the right place is no less important than getting within range in the first place.

Once you've placed yourself within range of a deer—for some archers twenty yards, for others fifty—you should make the shot with assurance. As successful bowhunter Stan Chiras said, "The work should be in finding the animal and planning a setup. Once he's within range, making the shot should be a foregone conclusion." That doesn't mean you'll never miss a good shot (every experienced bowhunter has and will), but you must feel confident about the outcome. If you don't, your shooting needs work.

Solid shooting form, developed and honed at the target butt, is the source of that confidence. You might ask what shooting targets has to do with hunting, and I'd answer, "Everything." If you haven't mastered the shooting basics, you won't perform well under the stress of hunting. That's what this chapter covers—the basics of form, the foundation that will make you a good hunting archer. As the late Al Henderson, 1976 Olympic archery coach and an avid hunter, said, "It may be more important for hunters to practice form than for target shooters because in the field you're shooting under totally uncontrollable conditions—fatigue, weather, hunger, tough positions. You have to concentrate 100 percent on aiming and holding on that animal, and you have to entrust your physical form to practice."

I couldn't agree more. If you have shooting basics and form down pat, you'll perform well automatically when the time comes.

Relaxation

Before going through the steps of good form, I want to emphasize the foundation of all good shooting—relaxation. Philosophies have changed over the years, as we can see from Saxton Pope's advice on shooting a bow in *Hunting with the Bow and Arrow*, written in 1923: "Having observed all the prerequisites of good shooting, nothing so insures a keen, true arrow flight as an effort of supreme tension during the release. The chest is held rigid in a position of moderate inspiration, the back muscles are set and every tendon is drawn into elastic strain; in fact, to be successful, the whole act should be characterized by the utmost vigor."

That was probably standard advice then, but today, most professionals would tell you to strike words like "tension," "rigid," "strain," and "vigor" from your archery vocabulary. That's partly because the reduced holding weight of the compound bow reduces strain and tension. But it goes far beyond that; many traditional archers also advocate an easy, fluid, tension-free style.

That's because relaxed, natural form eliminates many of the variables created by muscle tension. Duplicating muscle tension exactly, shot after shot, is nearly impossible. If you relax, however, your body will assume the same natural position each shot. The result is consistency. Relaxed form also cuts down on fatigue and reduces injuries.

Shooting Basics

This section explains the fundamentals of good form. When starting out, concentrate on each element. Shooting lots of arrows as fast as possible is not the way to learn quickly. If anything, it will only ingrain bad habits, and you'll spend the rest of your archery life trying to unlearn them. Start out deliberately, performing each step slowly and mechanically, thinking about each one in turn. After a few practice sessions they'll become second nature, and you'll do them automatically.

Stance

Stand at a ninety-degree angle to the target, feet shoulder width apart. Now step back a half step with the front foot and pivot slightly toward the

Good shooting begins with a solid stance. Assume that the target is directly in line with the photographer. You can see that I have a slightly open stance, a good starting point because it gives good clearance between your bow arm and the bow string. Start with your feet shoulder width apart and your weight evenly distributed on both feet.

target to form a slightly open stance, feet still shoulder width apart. This is a good basic starting point, which you might adjust later. Keep your weight evenly distributed on both feet, and stand straight. Don't lean forward or back. As you raise the bow to shoot, your stance should remain unchanged. You should not lean to pull the bow or cock your head to the side to line up the sights. You want to fit the bow to your natural stance, not contort your body to fit the bow.

Bow Hand Placement

Any slight variation in hand placement can change the angle of your bow and throw arrows off target, so place your hand carefully. Major pressure should be on the meaty part of the thumb. That gives you a "low" wrist, meaning your wrist is bent downward, not straight or cocked upward. As Al Henderson said, "With a relaxed, natural wrist, you don't have to control the wrist and the bow. It naturally falls into the same position every time. That's why I teach the natural, low-wrist position."

Avoid palming the bow, which creates two pressure points—the thumb and the heel of the hand. There should be only one pressure point, the meaty part of the thumb. To ensure that, rotate your bow hand slightly (about one-eighth turn) off vertical. That's the ideal hand angle because it's the most natural position. To see what I mean, raise your arm and

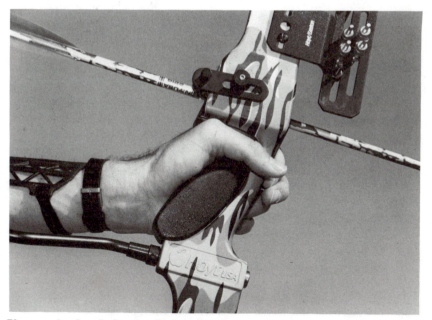

Place your hand on the bow handle so pressure is centered on the meaty part of the thumb about halfway between the second and third joints.

point at a distant object with your index finger. If you're relaxed, your hand will not be vertical, but turned slightly. That's the same natural angle you want on the bow handle, because it eliminates bow torque. If you force your hand into a vertical position, it will rotate after the shot and twist the bow to the side. With your bow hand in this relaxed position, your little finger will not hang in front of the bow handle but to the side. This is a good way to check for correct hand position.

As you draw the bow, continually check your bow hand. You often see a hunter with the fingers of his bow hand extended stiffly or gripping the bow like he's choking a snake. Tension like that torques the bow. That's bad. The fingers of your bow hand should be relaxed, hanging loosely throughout the shot. Concentrate on keeping a loose bow hand.

String Hand Placement

The most common string grip, which I suggest for beginners, is called the Mediterranean grip. It consists of holding the bow with three fingers on the string, the index finger above the arrow, and the third and fourth

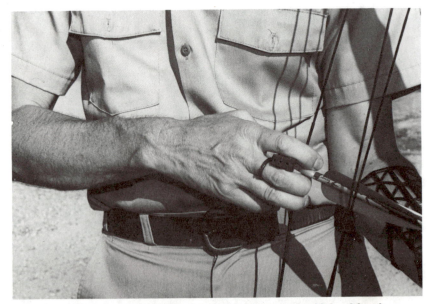

Start with a split-finger grip, the index finger above the arrow, the third and fourth fingers below. The string hand should be rotated one-eighth turn off vertical in a natural position, and the wrist should be straight.

It's important to remain relaxed at full draw. When your bow hand is turned in a natural position, your fingers should be relaxed and loose and your little finger should never come in front of the bow handle.

fingers below the arrow. Hook the string on your fingers at the first joint, and as you do, keep your hand rotated slightly to the side in a natural position, just as you did your bow hand. If you hold your fingers absolutely vertical on the string, your hand will try to rotate back to a natural position as you draw, twisting the string and preventing a smooth release. (With a release aid, the angle of your hand will be dictated by the style of release you're using.)

The wrist on your drawing hand should remain straight. If you try to release with a crooked arm and hand, you must relax your entire arm before you can release the string. If your arm is straight from elbow to string fingers, it's relaxed from the start, and only your fingers need to relax to let the string go.

The Bow Arm

Al Henderson said the most important part of shooting is a relaxed bow arm, because the bow arm puts the arrow in the target. He said you can have an imperfect release, but if your bow arm is solid, the arrow will go in; if your bow arm is off, the most perfect release won't do. A good bow arm is critical, and that means it's absolutely relaxed.

Professional archery instructor Lonnie Jones said, "The bow arm is just a brace. Once you get the arm up and pull on the string, the arm locks into place. It can relax."

As your muscles develop, your arm will become very stable in this relaxed condition. Two other points about the bow arm are worth making. First, your shoulder should be pulled down, so your arm bone pushes directly into the shoulder socket, bone against bone. That's solid. If you hunch your shoulder up toward your chin, your bow arm will be much less solid. Second, as you hold your bow in the shooting position, rotate your arm so the inside of your elbow is vertical for maximum string clearance. If the inside of your elbow faces up, you'll probably end up with painful string welts on your arm.

Drawing the Bow

With correct stance, your hands placed carefully, and your bow arm raised into shooting position, you're ready to draw the bow. To do that, you might find it helpful to keep the elbow on your drawing arm high to give you better leverage. But above all, remember to pull with your back muscles, not your biceps.

As you draw, the greatest pressure should be applied to your middle finger. Your index finger above the arrow, and your fourth finger should just "float" on the string. If you get blisters or heavy calluses on these

Draw your bow, pulling primarily with your back muscles, and maintain a natural stance with your weight distributed evenly on both feet. Do not lean forward or back. Particularly note my bow arm here. The shoulder is pulled down to form a straight line from my neck to my hand. A stable bow arm is the key to accuracy.

fingers, you're pulling too hard with them. Lighten up, and let your middle finger do the work.

The string anchor point is a critical part of shooting. It has to be solid, and it has to be consistent from one shot to the next. You can anchor any number of ways, but with fingers, I suggest you start by anchoring

When shooting with fingers, the most common anchor point is the tip of the index finger in the corner of the mouth. The wrist should be straight, and most of the pressure should be applied to the middle finger as the index and fourth fingers "float" on the string. Notice the finger spacer on the finger tab that prevents pinching of the arrow nock.

You can anchor various ways with a release aid. Using a wrist-strap model, I anchor with the big knuckle of my index finger planted solidly behind my jaw bone. A string peep serves as a second anchor "check." Release by slowly squeezing the trigger; never punch it.

When using a finger-held release, this hunter anchors with his index finger under his jaw.

with the tip of your index finger in the corner of your mouth. That's probably the most common. Some people prefer to anchor by placing the big thumb knuckle under the chin. Whichever anchor point you choose, be consistent with it.

How you anchor with a release aid depends on the style of aid you use. With a wrist-strap release, I anchor by placing the big knuckle of my thumb solidly behind my jaw bone. With finger-held releases, most shooters anchor by pressing the back of the hand or the big knuckle of the index finger into the jaw. Nothing says you have to anchor any exact way. Just choose a solid, comfortable anchor point, and be consistent with it.

The Release

The next step is to release the arrow using either your fingers or a release aid. To release smoothly with fingers, simply relax them and let the string slip away. Lonnie Jones suggests that you forget about your fingers. If you focus on them, you'll deliberately open them to let go of the string, an action guaranteed to produce a bad shot. Instead, concentrate on your drawing-arm elbow, lifting up and back as if pushing against a wall. As

Check hand position before shooting. Both hands are turned one-eighth turn to the side in a natural, relaxed position. All pressure on the bow hand is applied to the meaty part of the thumb. Your body from your bow hand through your shoulders to the elbow on your drawing arm should be nearly in line. To release the string, continue to "push back" with your elbow as your string fingers relax.

you "push," allow your string fingers to relax. Suddenly the string will slip away smoothly. "Don't let go of the string," Jones advises. "Let the string go. There's a big difference." You should be almost surprised when the bow goes off, as you are by the bang of a rifle when you slowly squeeze the trigger.

With a relaxed release, your hand moves straight back, close to your face, and your fingers are limp and relaxed. If your fingers are stiff, you've opened your hand deliberately to get rid of the string. If your hand moves out to the side of your face, you've plucked the string. If it moves forward, you let your hand follow the string. These are all bad. With each shot, make sure your hand moves back along your face and your fingers are relaxed.

You must also relax when using a release aid. Never punch the trigger; rather, squeeze slowly until the string is gone. Shooting with a release aid

As your string fingers relax, the string will slip away and your string hand should move straight back close to your face. The fingers should be relaxed, not stiff. After the shot, continue to aim at the target (follow through). Your bow should move very little.

should be just like squeezing the trigger on a bench-rest rifle. You should be surprised, even startled, when the bow goes off. Again, your hand should move straight back sharply in reaction to the shot.

Follow-through

After the shot, continue to aim at the target. Your bow should move very little, and your sights should be nearly on target. If the bow jerks violently, you've shot with tension. Try adjusting your alignment by opening or closing your stance. And work on your bow hand, bow arm, and string arm to eliminate any tension that could be torquing the bow or throwing it to the side. All motion should be in direct line toward the target, not to the side.

Practice Shooting Form

You aren't born with relaxed shooting ability. It comes with practice under controlled conditions, so spend plenty of time on the practice range. At

All good shooting starts with good form. To work on relaxed form, stand close to
your target butt and practice shooting with your eyes closed. This allows you to concentrate
strictly on shooting basics. The Saunders Indian Cord Grass Matt is a good all-around
target butt for practice.

twenty yards or so, go through the above steps over and over, until they
become natural and automatic.

Here's one tip that might help you learn good form — try practicing
with your eyes closed. (Stand close to the target butt so you don't miss.)
First check your stance and hand placement. Then draw, aim, and close
your eyes. Now, before releasing, mentally check your body. Is your bow
hand relaxed, fingers loose? Is your bow arm relaxed, the shoulder pulled
down? Is your string hand straight, major pressure on the middle finger?
Are you pulling with your back? If everything feels good, begin to relax
your string fingers (or slowly squeeze the trigger on your release). After the
shot, keep your eyes closed and mentally check your stance. Has your
string hand moved straight back? Are your string fingers loose and relaxed? Is your bow hand still relaxed? Now open your eyes. Are you still
aiming at the target? You should be. Practice this way regularly, running
through the check points before and after each shot. With closed eyes, you
can forget about aiming to concentrate totally on developing solid form.

Aiming

Sight Picture

Time-worn advice has always been to "pick a spot" on an animal. With instinctive (no sights) shooting, that may be valid. But with sights, that isn't necessary, because most sight shooters don't focus on the animal at all, but rather on the sight itself. In essence, the sight becomes the "spot," in place of a spot on the animal. It's important to make this distinction because you can't focus on both sight and target at the same time, especially at longer distances. To aim correctly, you must know where you're focusing.

Tim Strickland, a top-rated professional target archer and hunter, said he learned aiming principles from competitive pistol shooting, in which you concentrate on the sights and blur the target. "On animals I look at the aperture, not the animal," he said. "It's a lot easier to correct errors by focusing on what you're shooting *with* than what you're shooting *at*."

For me, focusing on the sight helps in another way. The hardest part of bare-bow shooting, in my opinion, is picking a spot on an animal under the tension of hunting. Your mind can go blank, and you can just fire off into the air somewhere without aiming. I've done it. Using sights and concentrating on a pin rather than the deer gives you a much more positive reference. You don't pick a spot on the animal, but a sight pin. You're far less likely to get buck fever concentrating on that pin than on the animal.

Relaxed Aiming

Tim Strickland brings out some interesting points about bow movement and precise aiming. His experience comes not only from hunting but from the target line, where precision is measured in fractions of an inch. "If your sight never moved, you'd have no problems with accuracy," says Strickland. "But the sight does move. It's always going through what I call an arc of motion [off target and back again]. You can't stop that.

"The secret to accuracy is learning not to fight that motion. The more you force, trying to hold dead center on the target, the worse you'll shoot. When you try to do better than you're able, you do worse. The reason you don't always shoot in the center is that you're consciously trying to make corrections. The idea is to relax and let your instincts work. Your eye and mind always seek center, and if you just leave things alone, the sight will move back to the center. This is a form of instinctive shooting."

Strickland deals with motion in a couple of specific ways. First, he puts drops of glue on his sight pins to enlarge them to about one-eighth inch in diameter, and he paints them fluorescent colors.

"The larger the pins, the less they seem to move," he said. "It's more important to reduce the perception of movement than to use tiny pins, because you can't hold any tighter with small pins, anyway. The idea is to reduce the feeling of movement. Don't worry if you can't see around the pin. Just let it cover the target."

Second, he never stops his release or jerks back on target once he's started a shot. "Once you've started your shot, never stop and try to correct your sight picture. That only makes things worse. Even if you release the string the instant your sight covers the middle of the target, you'll be off by the time the arrow leaves the bow. You actually have a better chance of hitting the center if your pin has moved off and you keep your motion going, because where is it going next? You're always unconsciously bringing the sight back to the center, so don't fight it. Just release smoothly. The test in mastering aiming is whether you can begin and complete a shot without stopping because of pin movement. Just start your shot, and execute your form, and let the bow do what it wants to do."

A big block of Styrofoam like this makes an excellent broadhead target. This particular target is an old float out of a houseboat.

Practice
Home Practice Ranges

For backyard shooting, you can choose from several styles of target butts. The most common is three bales of hay. If the bales are tight, you can just stack them on top of each other and they'll stop arrows fine. Make sure you have a good backstop, such as a solid wood fence or a sheet of plywood, because arrows may go through, especially if they hit cracks between the bales. If the bales are loose, band them together to tighten them up. Cedar bales are even better than hay.

You can make a good backstop by stacking cardboard and banding it together so you're shooting into the cut edges. Many pro shops make permanent backstops in their shooting ranges this way. It's effective and cheap. I also know of clubs that buy baled cardboard from department stores and use these bales as backstops. You can get a lot of shooting out of a cardboard bale.

Commercial target matts are more convenient. I use the Saunders' Indian Grass Matt and find it convenient and reliable. For handy use in your yard or in the field, twenty-five- or thirty-inch models are fine, but for a permanent range where you shoot long distances, the fifty-inch matt is great. You can get a wheeled stand to move this target easily. If you have a hard time pulling arrows from these targets, use a Saunders arrow puller, a small rubber pad that gives you a good grip on the shaft. Carbon arrows are especially hard to pull.

Some target butts consist of a burlap shell filled with cotton batting or similar loose fill. These stop arrows very well, and the arrows are easy to remove. They make excellent backyard target butts.

Foam matts are okay, but they don't last as long; they leave residue on the arrows, and they're hard to pull arrows from. I think they're better for temporary use around camp than they are for constant shooting in a backyard range.

Field Practice

With the above regimen, you'll develop a style that will serve you well on the target range or under the roughest hunting conditions. But to get the most from that style, you have to adapt it to hunting situations. You can begin on the target range by shooting from various positions — kneeling, sitting, or bent over as if you were shooting around a tree. You can also climb onto your roof and shoot down into your yard to learn how to shoot from different angles.

Good form must be adapted to field conditions. Systematically practice awkward angles and stances to prepare for hunting, but always apply the principles of good form learned at the target butt.

Many tournaments are designed with bowhunters in mind. If possible, take part in trail shoots and 3-D animal shoots. Most local clubs put on several such events each year. At a higher level, tournaments organized by the International Bowhunting Organization (IBO) are set up the same way, and the competition reaches a very high level. At these events, distances are unmarked, and realistic animal targets are placed in natural settings, so conditions closely simulate hunting. That, combined with the pressure of competition (similar to the pressure of shooting animals at close range), makes these competitions excellent preparation for hunting.

Finally, practice in the field. Roving and stump shooting are terms that have been around for years, and they're still valid today. They refer to a style of practice where you simply walk around the woods and shoot at rotten stumps, pine cones, limbs — whatever catches your eye and offers a challenging target. You soon learn to judge range and shoot from awkward positions, and you learn your limitations, so you know when to shoot and when to hold off for a better angle.

This is my favorite form of practice because it's almost like hunting. To carry it a step further, I always carry two blunt-tipped practice arrows in my eight-arrow hunting quiver. During any hunt, I shoot regularly during lulls in the action. Walking back to camp on a trail, I shoot at stumps and cones along the trail to keep my eye sharp and my muscles loose. These practice arrows are every bit as important as my hunting arrows.

6

Tuning Your Bow

A friend of mine often berated himself for making bad shots. He blamed himself for plucking the string, dropping his bow arm, losing concentration, failing to pick a spot. Yet, he had good form and control. He was a good archer.

Looking at his tackle, I could see some major discrepancies. His quiver contained different-sized arrow shafts and different weights and styles of broadheads. His arrow rest was flimsy. He thought these "little" things were irrelevant, but I thought many of his bad shots were the result of mismatched, inconsistent tackle, not poor shooting.

One of the popular archery buzzwords these days is bow "tuning," which is the process of adjusting your bow for the best performance and accuracy. Some archers make too big a deal of it and work themselves into a sweat over irrelevant details, while others overreact against the very idea and refuse to do anything even remotely technical. The ideal attitude lies somewhere between these two extremes. Most of us are hunters first and archers second. We don't want to spend all our time fiddling with tackle. At the same time, we want to succeed and make clean kills. To do those things, our arrows must fly true. That's the purpose of tuning. It's not complicated; a few simple procedures will give you good arrow flight, which is important not only for accuracy but for penetration too. A straight-flying arrow will penetrate far better than one flying crooked.

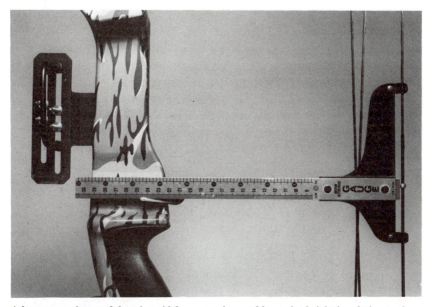

A bow square is a useful tuning aid for measuring nocking point height in relation to the arrow rest. For finger shooting, place the nock set about half an inch above horizontal. For shooting with a release aid, start with the nock set even with the arrow rest.

For tuning, you will need a bow square and Allen wrenches to fit the adjustable parts of your bow. A bow scale, although not essential, can be useful. For gauging arrow clearance, buy a can of spray powder (deodorant or foot powder). And, of course, you need a target butt to shoot into.

Matched Tackle

For your tackle to shoot accurately and consistently, the spine of your arrows must be matched to your bow, and all your arrows must weigh the same. Matched tackle is the starting point for bow tuning, since varied spine and arrow weight will change arrow flight significantly.

To improve consistency in your shots, your arrows must have the right length and spine for your bow (see chapter 2), and your heads must all weigh the same. You probably won't notice a variation of four or five grains in head weight, but you should definitely see the effects of ten grains variance. That much weight not only changes the weight of your arrows enough to make them shoot high or low, but it affects the spine value of the arrow. Try to standardize all your arrows. Once you've found a combina-

tion of shaft size, fletching style, and head weight that works for you, stick
with it.

For easiest tuning, use an arrow rest you can move in and out to
adjust center shot. You can use a solid, one-piece rest and get acceptable
arrow flight, but one-piece rests have their limitations. A rest that cushions
the arrow both vertically and horizontally offers the most potential. To
summarize what I've said under "Arrow Rests" in chapter 3, a flipper/
plunger works best with fingers, a shoot-through with a release aid.

Preliminary Settings

For simplicity's sake, all directions here are for right-handed shooters. If
you shoot left-handed, do the opposite.

Tiller

Tiller is the distance between the bow limbs and the string. With recurves
and longbows, the bottom limb is a quarter- to a half-inch closer to the

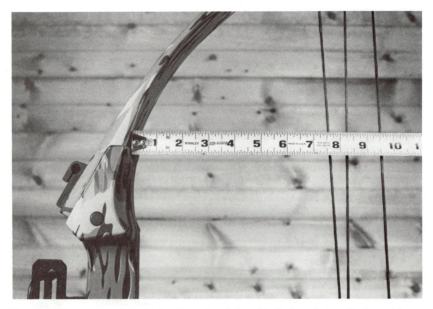

To gauge tiller, measure from limbs where they fit into the limb pockets to the bow string.
On a compound bow, tiller can be set dead even. If you change draw weight, make
sure you turn each limb bolt the same amount, or you'll change tiller—and nocking point
height.

string than the top, and this is a critical measurement. With compounds it isn't so critical, so I suggest you start with even tiller. That is, the top and bottom limbs will be exactly the same distance from the bow string. You can gauge this by measuring (with a tape or ruler) from the limbs — right where they fit into the limb pockets — to the bow string. To alter tiller and bring it to dead even, turn one of the limb bolts. After adjusting the limbs to even tiller, anytime you change bow weight turn both limb bolts exactly the same amount to avoid changing tiller. Tiller must remain constant, because changing tiller changes nocking-point height.

Nocking Point Height

Equip your bowstring with a clamp-on nockset (see chapter 3) for easy adjustment. If you shoot with fingers, clamp the nockset about a half-inch above a point ninety degrees from the rest (you measure this with the bow square). If you shoot with a release aid, place the nockset even with the rest. You might move it later, but these are good starting points.

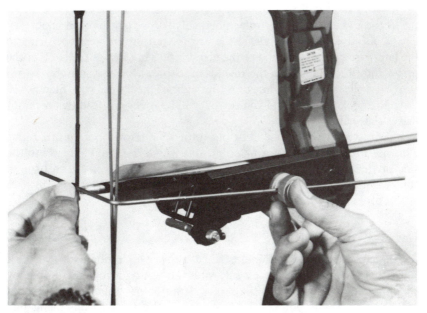

The Tru-Center Gauge made by Golden Key-Futura makes centering an arrow easy. You set the gauge against the side of your bow and slide a ring on the gauge to correspond with the string. Then you flip the gauge over and adjust your rest until the arrow lines up with the ring on the gauge.

Arrow Alignment

This one step can solve about 90 percent of arrow flight problems. This isn't mysterious. You can usually "eyeball" arrows into alignment. Golden Key-Futura makes a handy device called a True Center Gauge for centering arrows, but you can do the same thing visually by first finding the "string center" of the upper limb. On most compound bows, that isn't the exact center of the limb, because the string, as it loops around the wheel, is slightly to one side. To find the string center, measure the distance from the string, where it touches the wheel, to the side of the bow limb. Let's say it's three-fourths inch. Now, just above the handle, make a mark on the limb three-fourths inch from the side of the limb (this assumes the limb is the same width here as at the tip).

With the bow limb marked, stand the bow in a corner or rest it against a chair, and nock an arrow. Next, visually line up the bow string with the centering mark you've made on the limb, so they're in exact line, and, without moving your head, look at the arrow to see its relationship with the string. If you shoot with a release aid, the arrow should be in a direct line with the string. That is, you should not be able to see the arrow tip on either side of the string.

If you shoot with fingers, you should be able to see the entire arrow tip to the left of the string (remember, this is for right-handed shooters). That's because, when you release the string, your fingers push the string to the left, forcing the nock end of the arrow left. That brings the back of the arrow into direct line with the front, launching the arrow straight. If you start with the arrow tip in line or to the right of the string, your fingers will force the nock end left, and your arrow will be flying crooked the instant it leaves the string.

Adjust your arrow rest in or out until your arrow lines up just right. This need to center your arrow points out why a rest stuck directly to the side of the bow often gives terrible arrow flight. If you insist on using a solid plastic rest, mount it on an adjustable plate so you can line up your arrow properly with the string.

Gauging Arrow Flight

Setting up your bow as I've described above will probably solve most tuning problems. To some extent, you can gauge arrow flight just by watching your arrows fly to the target. If an arrow wobbles badly, you'll see the erratic flight. You may be able to make the needed adjustments just from that, and you may be satisfied without going any further.

But that's a by-guess-and-by-golly method. To tune more precisely, you need a better way to "read" arrow flight. The easiest and quickest way

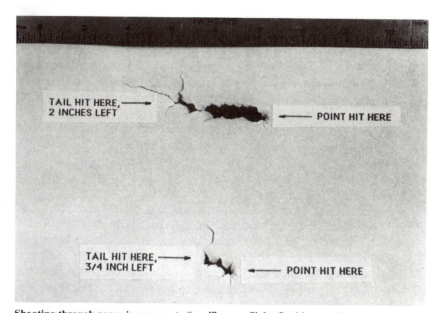

TAIL HIT HERE, ——→
2 INCHES LEFT

←—— POINT HIT HERE

TAIL HIT HERE, ——→
3/4 INCH LEFT

←—— POINT HIT HERE

Shooting through paper is one way to "read" arrow flight. In this case, the top arrow, shot from a distance of five yards, tore a two-inch horizontal hole, indicating an undesirable amount of fishtailing. After a slight arrow-rest adjustment, the arrow tore a hole only three-fourths of an inch long on the bottom shot. The bottom hole indicates acceptable arrow flight.

is shooting through paper. With this method (as opposed to bare-shaft tuning methods), you can tune with your broadhead hunting arrows. It doesn't require the ability to shoot tight groups. You're strictly judging arrow flight.

All you need is a frame to hold the paper, tape to hold the paper on the frame, and paper to shoot through. Old magazine or newspaper pages work fine. I made a frame by cutting a rectangular hole through a cardboard box to form a window through the box.

Set up the frame in front of your target butt and tape a piece of paper tightly over the window. Stand about five yards away and shoot an arrow with a field tip through the paper. If your bow is perfectly tuned, the arrow will make nothing but a round hole with fletching cuts around it through the paper.

If it's not perfectly tuned, the arrow will fly sideways to some degree and will tear a long hole through the paper. You can read the tear, because the field point makes a round hole, and the tail leaves fletching cuts.

Common Problems

Porpoising

If your arrow tears a vertical rip in the paper, you know your arrow is wobbling up and down like the tail of a swimming porpoise, or "porpoising," a problem that should be corrected first. Porpoising is caused by improper nocking point height. To correct it, move the nockset down if the arrow is fletching high, or move the nockset up if the arrow is fletching low.

Fishtailing

When an arrow wobbles from side to side, it is said to be "fishtailing." The amount of wobble is affected by arrow spine, lateral position of the arrow rest, spring tension in the cushion plunger, and possibly other variables. Fishtailing is indicated by a horizontal tear in the paper.

If the arrow is fletching left, it is weak in spine. To correct it, increase spring tension of the cushion plunger, move the rest to the left, decrease bow draw weight, use a lighter head, use stiffer arrow shafts, increase the amount of fletching, shorten the arrows (if possible), or switch to a mechanical release.

If the arrow is fletching right, it is too stiff. To correct it, decrease the spring tension of the plunger button, move the rest to the right, increase bow draw weight, use a heavier head, use weaker-spined shafts, use less fletching, or shoot longer arrows.

Continue to make these adjustments until your arrows are flying well at five yards, then move back to ten or fifteen yards to check them again. You should still be getting clean tears. (Do this on a calm day. Wind nullifies your testing.)

Don't worry if you can't get perfect bullet holes through the paper every time. If you can reduce the tear in any direction to an inch or less, your bow is shooting better than 90 percent of the bows in the field — and good enough to kill deer cleanly. This testing is simply a way to eliminate major errors and ensure good arrow flight.

Fletching Contact

If you've followed these steps and still get lousy arrow flight, check for fletching contact. Bad arrow flight often results from arrow contact with the bow. Arrows must clear the bow cleanly to fly well, especially if they have plastic vanes. If vanes smash into the rest or the side of the bow, the erratic arrow flight will be obvious, and you won't be able to correct it with the above tuning steps. If fletching contact is your problem, you'll see plastic streaks (from the vanes) on the bow window or arrow rest.

To judge contact, spray your bow window, arrow rest, and vanes with dry-powder deodorant. (Sprinkle-on powder doesn't work; it just blows around.) Now shoot the sprayed arrow and inspect the sprayed areas on the bow and fletching. Any contact will produce very clear marks in the

Vane contact with the arrow rest can be a cause of poor arrow flight. The nocks on your arrows should be turned to assure maximum fletching clearance. The bottom vane on this arrow is lined up to pass midway between the two support arms on a Star Hunter rest.

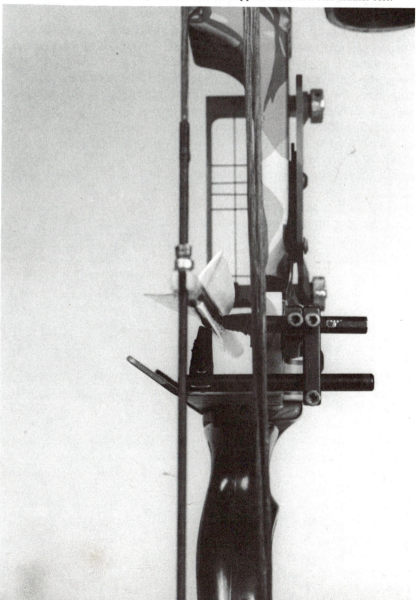

powder. If there are no marks, count your blessings. And don't worry about minor contact. You could spend weeks on this and never get perfection. If you see only slight marks where a vane brushed the rest, and your arrows are flying well through the paper, don't worry about it. You're ready for hunting.

If there are severe marks, your arrows or rest needs some adjustment. Make sure your rest is set for maximum clearance. On a shoot-through rest, adjust the arms as far apart as possible without letting the arrow fall through. With a flipper or springy rest, cut off as much of the arrow support arm as possible without having the arrow tumble off the rest.

Then sight down your arrows to see how the fletching lines up. To do this, place an arrow on the string and sight down the arrow to see where the vanes lie closest to the side of the bow or the rest. The vanes should be tilted in just the right direction for maximum clearance. If they aren't, the best solution is to remove the nocks on the arrows and replace them with new nocks, glued on at the right angle for maximum clearance. If your bow and arrows are well matched and tuned, you should be able to achieve nearly total clearance just by turning the nocks. Once you've found the right nock position, glue all your nocks on the same way.

With modern arrow rests and cutout risers, getting good clearance should not be a major problem. If you shoot a bow with a thick wood handle or a solid plastic rest, getting total clearance can be nearly impossible, and feather fletching may be your only salvation. The feathers will still hit, but they won't throw the arrow off course.

Following these simple procedures should help you get excellent arrow flight and shoot tight groups. Good tuning allows you to make the most of your shooting ability.

7

Taking Care of Tackle

Bows are durable and reliable when given reasonable care, so you'll probably have to do few repairs. In twenty years of bowhunting—ten with a recurve and ten with a compound—I've had bow trouble only one time. On that occasion, I was crossing a boulder field, when a boulder as big as a house started to roll under me. I jumped off and fell on my bow, breaking the limb tip. That was my only bow problem, ever.

Nevertheless, some care can extend the life of your bow and prevent disasters. And certainly you'll damage some arrows that will need repair. Included in this chapter are some tips to keep your tackle working efficiently under all conditions.

Bow Care

Dry Firing

Shooting a bow with no arrow on the string, or dry firing, is one of the worst things you can do to a bow. When you shoot a bow with an arrow, the arrow absorbs much of the bow's energy, up to 80 percent. If you shoot the bow with no arrow on the string, 100 percent of the released energy vibrates through the bow itself, and the results can be disastrous. The stress can break the handle, limbs, cables, or string. Never dry fire a bow.

Shooting very light arrows is tantamount to dry firing, because the light arrow absorbs too little of the bow's energy. To prevent damage to your bow, use reasonably heavy arrows. A good guideline is to shoot at least 7 grains of arrow weight for every pound of bow weight. That is, if your draw weight is 60 pounds, you should shoot arrows of at least 420 grains (7 grains x 60 pounds = 420 grains). Using heavier arrows is okay, because the added arrow weight makes your bow more efficient (although beyond 9 grains per pound of bow weight, your arrows will be needlessly slow), but using lighter arrows could damage your bow.

Heat and Moisture

A friend of mine once left his bow in a VW bus on a sunny day. The next time he drew the bow, the limbs split into a dozen pieces. Heat is hard on bows, particularly laminated wood limbs. The worst thing you can do is to lock your bow in the trunk of a car or hang it in a window rack on a sunny day. Keep the bow in a padded case out of the sun. Glass limbs withstand heat better, although one bow manufacturer told me glass limbs will also take a set, or become permanently bent, if left in hot conditions too long.

Moisture can seep between the laminations on wooden bows and delaminate the limbs. An occasional rainstorm isn't much to worry about, but if you're hunting with a wood-limbed bow in constant rain for days on end, you should dry your bow occasionally. Glass limbs are fairly impervious to moisture.

Some of the worst bow damage can occur in transport, as the bow slides around in the bed of a pickup or vibrates in a window rack. To prevent needless wear, keep your bow in a case. For general hunting, a soft, padded case with pockets for accessories is the most compact and convenient. Hard cases for compound bows are bulky, so they're less than ideal for everyday use. However, for flying on a commercial airline, a hard case is essential. If you plan to fly to hunting areas, buy a good plastic or aluminum case. Check the hinges and lock for quality, as these are the main weaknesses I've seen in hard cases.

String Repair

When my friend Roger Iveson drew his bow and shot at a mule deer, the string exploded. He has no idea where his arrow went, except that it didn't hit the deer. Upon inspection, he discovered he'd accidentally cut several strands of the bow string, probably with a broadhead, and the stress of shooting was enough to break it. Fortunately, his bow held together, and he was able to resume hunting after replacing the string.

That's the most likely accident you face in the field. Wax your string regularly with beeswax or special bow string wax, and inspect the string and cables regularly. A partially frayed strand isn't serious, but if the string is badly frayed or cut, replace it. You should always carry a spare string in the field, set up exactly like the one on your bow, and you should know how to replace it (if your bow has Fast Flight cables, you should also carry spare cables, because you can replace them just as you do a string). If the string on your bow is still intact, you can draw the bow and use a bowstringer (see your archery dealer for various styles) to hold the bow in a relaxed position while you change the string. If the string breaks completely, your only recourse is to loosen the limbs by backing out the limb bolts.

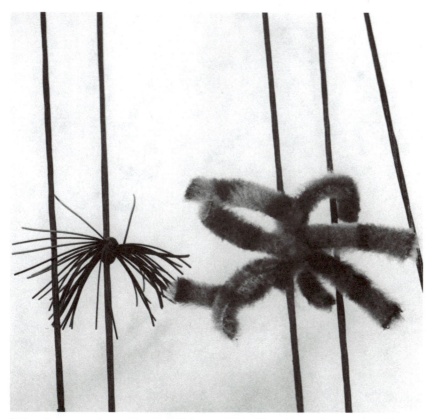

String silencers, such as rubber Catwhiskers and PolarFleece Tarantulas, dampen string vibration and make a bow much quieter.

Your hunting pack should include Allen wrenches to fit not only the limb bolts, but all other parts on your bow, so you can pull in-field maintenance on your sight, quiver, rest, or other parts.

Silencing a Bow

If sight and quiver screws don't have lock washers, I back the mounting plates with strips of inner-tube rubber, which acts not only as a lock

At close range, big game animals can hear an arrow sliding across a rest. Cover your rest to eliminate all sound. This Star Hunter is coated with Bear's Hair for silence.

washer to hold things tight, but as a dampener for noise. You should silence your bow in all ways possible. All animals can jump the string— bolt at the sound of your bow. The quieter the bow, the less likely that potential. On the string, place silencers to dampen string vibration. The most effective and trouble free are catwhiskers, thin strips of rubber used for skirting on bass lures. First tie a strip of this material around the string. Then stretch it tight and cut off the end with a sharp knife or scissors to separate the individual strands.

To avoid alerting animals before the shot, try to eliminate all pre-shooting noises. To prevent clicking an arrow against your bow, pad the entire sight window and the edges of your sight where an arrow might hit. Self-adhesive bow-saddle material or moleskin works well. Some arrow rests squeak as you slide an aluminum arrow across them. If your rest has a wire arm, as flippers and springies do, slide Teflon tubing over that area. If you use a rest with metal arms, either cover the arms with shrink tubing or pad them with moleskin or Bear's Hair (a self-sticking, rug-like material made by Bear Archery to pad the shelves on recurve bows). I even go

A quality roller cable slide like the Saunders 4 x 4 will eliminate cable-guard squeaks.

so far as to wrap the metal nocksets on my strings with soft tape or moleskin to prevent clicking if I accidentally tap them as I'm nocking the arrow to shoot.

Standard plastic cable slides often squeak when the cable guard gets wet. To prevent that, you can replace the cable slide with a roller cable

Sharp broadheads mean clean kills. Here Doug Chase uses a file to touch up his Zwickey Deltas during a hunting trip.

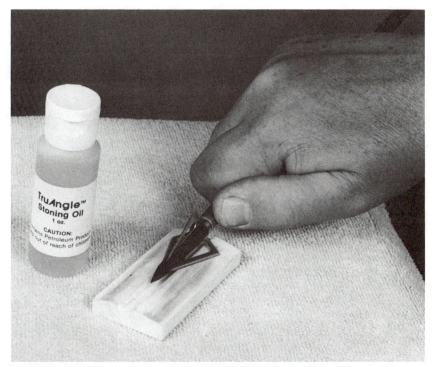

You can touch up mildly dull blades, even on replaceable-blade heads, with specialized sharpeners like this TruAngle Hone. The correct angle is built into the hone, so you simply slide the head back and forth to get a perfect edge.

slide like the Saunders 4 x 4, or you can cover the cable guard with a strip of Teflon tape, if you can find it.

To prevent wheels from squeaking, lubricate the axles occasionally. In dry conditions, spray them with a Teflon-based lubricant like Tri-Flon that won't collect dust. In wet weather use light oil like WD-40.

Arrow Care

Broadheads

Stainless steel heads won't rust in your quiver, but any heads containing carbon steel certainly will. To prevent that, coat them with light oil or petroleum jelly before pushing them into your quiver hood. Wash out the hood occasionally to get rid of dirt and grit that will dull the heads. To keep spare heads in good shape, push them into a block of Styrofoam.

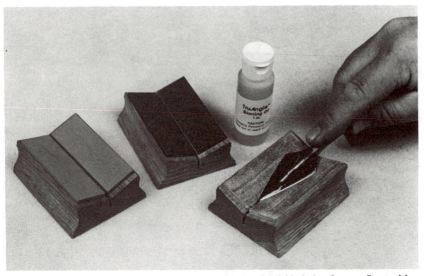

Sharpeners like these TruAngle Hones make sharpening fixed-blade heads easy. Start with the coarse grit, switch to fine, and finish on leather.

All broadheads can get dulled by oxidation, dust, and abrasion as you put them in and take them out of your quiver. Just because they were sharp at the start of the season doesn't mean they'll stay that way, so check them periodically and touch up any heads that are less than razor-sharp. With replaceable-blade heads you can replace just the blades, but that gets expensive and isn't really necessary unless the blades are badly damaged. You can easily sharpen broadheads with ceramic sharpeners called TruAngle Hones. These are made for either three- or four-blade heads. You don't have to worry about keeping proper blade angle because it's built into the stone. You simply slide the head back and forth along the hone, beginning with moderate pressure to start the edge and gradually reducing pressure to a light stroke to take off any wire edge.

To sharpen Zwickeys, Satellite Titans, or similar fixed-blade heads, start by filing the edges down to reduce the bevel. You can do this most easily by clamping a broadhead in a vise (wear leather gloves to prevent driving a broadhead through your finger in case you slip), and working them with a file. Try to maintain a constant angle with the file. Also, TruAngle and other companies make blocks with built-in files set at just the right angle. You just slide the head back and forth on the files. These automatically grind the correct angle on the broadhead.

Then you can finish the sharpening in a couple of ways. Bear makes a device called the Archer's Edge Broadhead Sharpener with two hardened-steel sharpening teeth. You simply slide the edge of the head between the teeth. Other companies make similar devices that do an acceptable job.

You can produce an even sharper edge by using actual stones, as you would with a knife. TruAngle makes sharpening blocks in coarse and fine grits especially for one-piece broadheads. Again, you just slide the heads over the stones, gradually reducing pressure to produce a smoother edge, starting with the coarse stone and finishing on the fine.

You also can sharpen one-piece heads on a whetstone, just as you would a knife. Start at the back edge of the blade and work to the tip, drawing the blade toward you as if you were shaving off a thin slice of the stone. Start with coarse grit and switch to fine. With all of these methods, finish up the edges with ceramic crock sticks or a sharpening steel. These will take off any fine wire edge or burrs left by the stone.

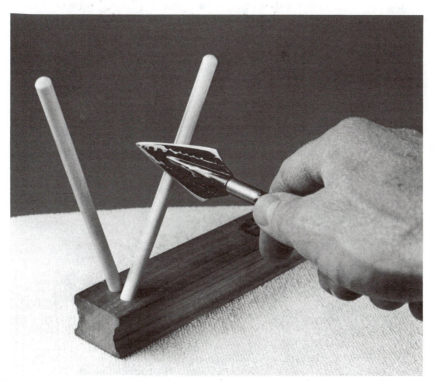

Apply the finishing touches with ceramic crock sticks or a steel. Maintain very light pressure to remove the wire edge and any small burrs.

Maintaining Shafts

Arrows are often bent in the quiver or during transport. A good quiver with sturdy grippers goes a long way toward protecting them as you hunt (see chapter 4).

In your car or on a horse, carry your arrows in a solid tube. Golden Eagle and other companies make good arrow cases. To make your own tube, cut a length of four-inch PVC pipe just longer than your arrows and glue a cap on one end. Slide a piece of foam rubber into that end to pad the tips. Fit the other end with a screw-on cap and cut a piece of foam for that end to pad the nock ends. A four-inch tube will hold eighteen arrows. For a more compact tube, use two- or three-inch pipe.

Graphite shafts don't bend, of course, but aluminum and wooden ones do, so you should know how to straighten them. To straighten arrows by hand, lay the bend of the arrow over the heel of your hand and flex the shaft opposite the direction of the bend. To test for subtle bends, cradle the arrow between your thumbnail and your index finger and spin the shaft. A straight arrow will spin smoothly, but a bent section will thump up and down.

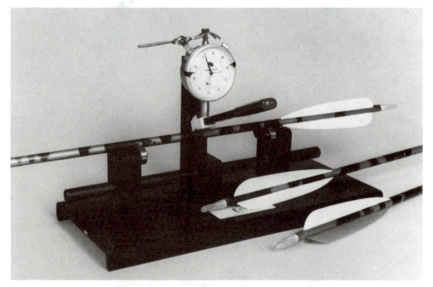

A precision arrow straightener like this Full Adjust Straightener, made in Lancaster, Pennsylvania, will restore arrows to virtually new condition. It can also be used to straighten broadheads.

For a more precise job, use a mechanical arrow straightener with a calibrated dial that reads minute bends. You straighten the arrow by applying pressure with a leverage arm, and this pressure can be controlled to avoid overbending. With practice, you can restore arrows to virtually new condition. If you shoot a lot, a precision arrow straightener is worth the money.

Shooting a cracked arrow can be dangerous. Inspect wooden and graphite arrows by flexing them in all directions, and if you see any slight cracks, throw them away. With aluminum arrows, impact dents and creases commonly occur as arrows smack into each other in a target butt. If the wall of the shaft is cracked or the shaft is kinked badly enough to crack when straightened, throw it away. Small creases or dents that don't break the shaft wall aren't a big concern.

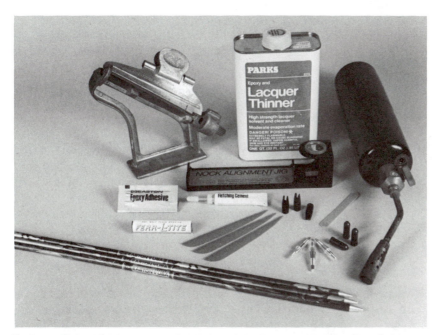

Basic supplies needed for arrowmaking. Left to right, from top: Fletching jig and clamp, nock alignment jig (optional, but good for assuring straight nocks), lacquer thinner (or similar solvent), heat source (propane torch), epoxy, fletching cement, nocks, emery board (or sandpaper), hot-melt glue, fletching, arrow inserts, screw-in broadhead adaptors (or screw-in heads), and arrow shafts.

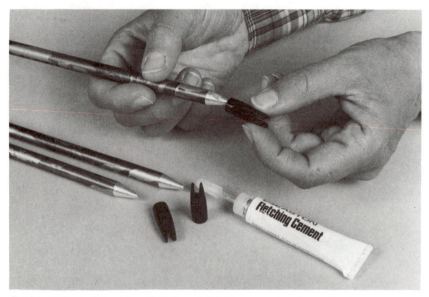

To glue nocks in place, put a small drop of fletching cement on the nock swage, turn the nock counterclockwise on the swage to spread the glue, and twist the nock clockwise to seat it firmly.

Nocks

If two arrows collide in a target butt, inspect the nocks. If you shoot an arrow with a cracked nock, the nock could split as you release, and the arrow could go any direction. Replace damaged nocks immediately. To remove an old nock, heat it in boiling water or a flame to soften it, and twist it off with pliers (be careful not to crimp the nock swage with the pliers). Then clean the nock swage with solvent and replace the nock as described below under Arrow Making.

Fletching

If you shoot through a vane with a field point, snip the hole out of the vane with scissors to smooth it out and go right on shooting. A broadhead hit will slice the vane, however, so you'll have to replace it. Feathers will wear out and need replacement. You can slice off old fletching with a sharp knife, but be careful not to cut into the shaft. Saunders makes an efficient fletching stripper. Carefully scrape off any old glue, clean the shaft with solvent, and replace the fletching as described below under Arrow Making.

Roughen the shaft in the fletching area with an emery board or sandpaper, swab the shaft with solvent to remove all dust and oil, and place the shaft in the fletching jig.

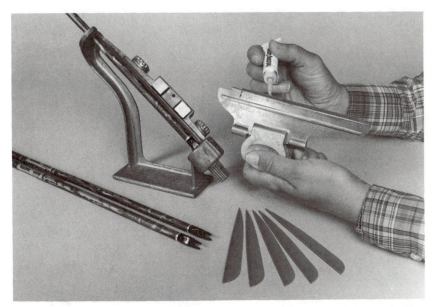

Place a vane or a feather in the fletching clamp and spread a thin bead of glue evenly along the full length of the base. Be sure to cover the base completely.

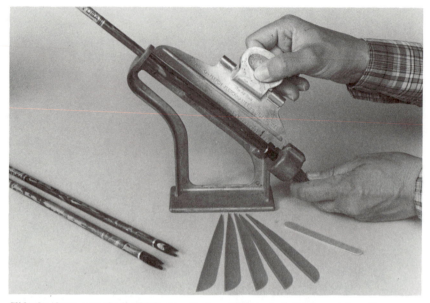

Slide the clamp onto the jig. Make sure the base of the vane is firmly seated on the arrow along its entire length, but don't press down hard enough to squeeze out all the glue.

After fletching, cut arrows to length. Never use a hacksaw or tube cutter. Use only a high-speed rotary saw to get a clean, square cut. If you can't afford a saw, have shafts cut at an archery shop.

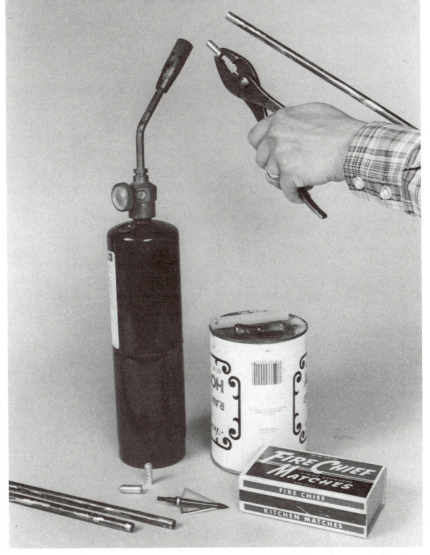

Install point inserts in the shaft. With aluminum inserts, use hot-melt glue. Install carbon inserts with epoxy.

Arrow Making

There are a number of benefits to making your own arrows. First, you can customize arrows to your needs. Store-bought arrows are all made the same way and may not be the best for your bow. The second advantage is quality. Store-bought arrows are mass produced and get little individual attention. By making your own, you can guarantee every arrow is made perfectly. Third, by learning how to make arrows, you learn how to repair them, which will save you time and money in the long run.

Making arrows is simple, because you actually don't make anything at all; you just assemble components—arrow shafts, nocks, fletching, fletching cement, hot-melt glue or epoxy, and point inserts. Useful supplies are coarse sandpaper, solvent (lacquer thinner or acetone), and paper towels. The only tools needed are a fletching jig and a rotary cutoff saw. If you can't afford a professional saw, take the shafts to a pro shop and have them cut. Martin Archery markets a hand saw that will do an acceptable job, too. A nock alignment tool is also handy for making precision arrows. The accompanying photos illustrate the arrow-making process.

8

Hunting Gear

Gear alone can't substitute for hunting and archery skills, but it can make you a better and more comfortable hunter. With all the gear available today, no hunter has any excuse for being less than prepared for all conditions. The right clothing, footwear, camouflage, hunting pack, optical gear, and scent products can make you a better hunter.

Clothing

I don't know if clothes make the man, but they can sure help make a bowhunter, because bowhunting requires close-range movement and enduring patience. Hunting clothes must first contribute to stealth, which means they must be quiet, camouflaged, and soft and flexible, so you can move without restriction.

Your clothing must also give you "staying power." Misery is a poor companion in bowhunting because it will make you quit. Anybody can hunt well on an Indian-summer day with a cool breeze blowing and golden aspen leaves whispering overhead. But what about in a blizzard? In rain? In wind? The outcome of a hunt often depends less on hunting ability than on staying power — your ability to hunt when hunting isn't fun. Even under terrible conditions, the right clothes can keep you hunting.

This net jacket is good for hunting on a hot summer day.

Hot Weather

If the weather is really hot, seventy degrees and up, as it often is during August mule-deer and antelope seasons and some southern bow seasons, net clothing is good because even a light breeze blows through the material to cool you. Just wear a T-shirt and underwear under net clothes. The worst thing you can do is slip net clothing over jeans. That defeats the whole purpose of the porous cloth. Spartan Realtree and other companies make good net clothing.

Super-light cotton clothes are nearly as good as net garments, but I stress the word "light." Many commercial cotton clothes are too heavy to breathe well. Two-ounce cotton is about right. It's thin enough that you can virtually read a book through it, yet it's surprisingly tough. Despite severe abuse, one pair of pants and a shirt my wife made have lasted me through five hunting seasons. The material is paper thin, which is good because the wind can blow right through to keep me cool. Hot-weather clothes must be porous. If you can't read through them, they're too heavy.

I only recommend cotton for hot weather hunting. It's okay then because it absorbs moisture (sweat) and it dries slowly, which helps to keep you cool. The lightweight materials discussed above are reasonably quiet. Materials with hard finishes, many of which are part nylon for durability, look good and wear like iron but they're noisy and won't soften with washing. That's not good.

Your head is your body's primary heat regulator. If you can keep your head cool, you'll go a long way toward keeping your body cool. Wear a cap with a bill to shade your face. A baseball cap is okay, but my favorite is a billed cap of T-shirt material made by Bob Fratzke. On really hot days, you can soak it with water, and it will cool your head effectively as the water evaporates.

Cool Weather

My first recommendation for hunting in cool weather is never to wear cotton. The very qualities that make cotton good in hot weather—high absorbancy and slow drying rate—will freeze you in the cold. Do yourself a favor and closet all your Levis, jockey shorts, and T-shirts—anything made of cotton—when cool weather arrives.

Underwear: For long johns, synthetics like polypropylene and Thermax are best. I've worn several brands of both and have found them good under varied conditions. They're soft for good movement, and rather than absorbing moisture, they wick moisture away from your skin so you feel dry, even shortly after a hard, sweaty hike. On one December mule deer hunt, I hiked hard to the top of a ridge, sweat pouring down, and then sat for an hour or two in bitter wind, glassing for deer. Surprisingly, I was comfortable. Sure, I felt clammy when I first stopped hiking, but within fifteen minutes my long johns were dry and comfortable. Cotton and even wool long johns, which dry slowly, can make you feel clammy for hours.

For vigorous hiking, the lightest synthetics are best for underwear. For active hunting, even in very cold weather, you'll rarely need heavier than medium weight. Expedition grades are best for stand hunting or for mountain climbing under severe conditions.

Knit acrylic is soft, flexible, and warm — hard to beat for cool-weather hunting. This hat and sweater are made by Bob Fratzke of Winona Mills. Wool gloves and scarf top off a good cold-weather outfit.

Outerwear: As much as I love wool, I have to vote for synthetics in outerwear, too. The most popular synthetics among bowhunters are polyester pile fabrics like PolarFleece and Arctic Fleece (I'll call these fleece) and knit acrylic, specifically, the camouflage knit garments made by Bob Fratzke of Winona Mills.

In general, synthetics are lighter than natural materials, and they absorb less water — about 1 percent of their own weight, according to manufacturers. Even when they get soaked, they don't get nearly as heavy as wool, and they dry more quickly. I've found that soaked fleece pants will dry in half an hour or so in the field, whereas wool pants take the better part of a day.

Synthetics are also durable. I've worn several fleece pants and shirts for several elk seasons, and they're still in great shape. I'd pit them against any wool pants. Fleece does melt, however, so you must keep it away from a crackling fire, or you'll end up with more holes than pants. Synthetics don't shrink so they always fit. They're much less abrasive than wool, so you can wear fleece or acrylic directly against your skin without rubbing yourself raw, and synthetics come in a variety of camouflage patterns.

In extreme cold — below zero — or in heavy wind, wool is still superior. Synthetics are porous and don't break the wind well. In really cold, late-season weather, I recommend wool Malone pants and a wool mackinaw.

On a normal day, I often wear a combination of synthetic clothes. I start with fleece pants (no long johns), a synthetic T-shirt, and an acrylic sweater. If the weather is really cold, I'll add lightweight polypropylene long johns and a fleece jacket.

Two other garments I normally carry are a down vest and rain gear. Browning's Down Stuff Vest, which stuffs into a compact sack and weighs only a few ounces, goes into my day pack. It offers instant warmth during rest breaks or sudden drops in temperature. The shell is noisy nylon, so I wear the vest under a sweater or a fleece jacket while hunting.

Most rain gear is anything but silent, but it can save you in a downpour. I consider it emergency gear, not hunting apparel. When rain is falling hard enough to force me to use rain gear, I'll probably bush up under a tree anyway. As standard emergency rain gear, I carry Browning's Superlight rain suit, made of urethane-coated nylon. It weighs next to nothing and rolls into a small carry sack. For extended hunting in the rain, I normally wear Gore-Tex rainwear made by Browning, Columbia Sportswear, or Remington. Some companies, such as Cabela's, sell rainwear with a fleece outer shell that is quieter than nylon.

For cold-weather stand hunting, start with the layers described above and then top off your outfit with insulated coveralls. Coveralls seal all the cracks to keep out a cold wind.

Head and Neck: Your head and neck are your major body-heat regulators, and keeping them warm helps to keep you warm overall. For cool and cold weather, knit hats are great. I far prefer Fratzke's knit acrylic hats and similar billed hats to the standard sock hat because the brim shades your eyes on sunny days and keeps the rain and snow off during bad weather, an especially good feature if you wear glasses.

Protecting your neck is important, too. A turtleneck sweater or long-john top works okay, but allows little heat regulation. A better choice is a knit scarf or a fleece jacket or knit sweater that zips up to form a turtleneck when needed, but can be zipped down for ventilation.

Hands: Except in very hot weather, I always wear gloves. The best I've found are wool army glove liners, available at most army surplus stores. They work well because they fit your hands snugly and don't interfere with shooting. You can slip a tab on right over the gloves or shoot with a release aid. Baggy cotton gloves, although good camouflage, can be more hindrance than help, and they'll freeze your hands when they get wet.

In severe cold, glove liners aren't enough. Thinsulate-lined Gore-Tex gloves are suitable for most conditions. Cabela's and Browning make good versions. You may have to slip these gloves off to shoot. For extreme cold, you may need to wear wool gloves inside insulated mittens to keep your hands warm enough to shoot.

Footwear

Proper footwear is also important for hunters. To prevent blisters, wear smooth, snug-fitting socks next to your feet and loose, bulky socks over these to absorb shock and moisture. Thin dress socks or liner socks made of polypropylene or Thermax work well next to your feet. Over these, standard wool socks are fine, although I've found that the newer synthetic socks, such as Remington's Thor-lo or Browning's polypropylene/wool, are far more durable.

For backpacking and carrying heavy meat loads, heavy leather boots with Vibram or similar lug soles are acceptable. Many come in insulated, Gore-Tex-lined versions. These are supposed to be absolutely waterproof, but I've worn at least fifteen different styles and have yet to find one that is. They're better than plain leather boots, but when hunting all day on a rainy day, you'll get wet feet.

In wet weather, boots with rubber bottoms and leather tops such as L. L. Bean's Maine hunting boots are a better choice. They have soft rubber soles that keep your feet dry and allow you to move quietly. A number of companies make similar boots. For severe cold weather or for sitting on a stand for long, cold hours, felt-lined pac boots are the best choice. Sorel and Browning are two of many companies that make good pacs.

For warm weather, lightweight canvas shoes or running-shoe-style hiking boots are good. They're lighter than regular boots, and many have softer soles. My favorite shoes are L. L. Bean's Maine canoe shoes, which have plain (unpadded) canvas tops and soft, rubber soles. They're sneaky, and they're inexpensive.

Camouflage

Clothing

Clothing must be soft and quiet. That's far more important than the color. Wearing camouflage clothing can add success to your hunt, however, as the right hue and pattern will enhance your efforts and give you confidence. So many good camouflage patterns have hit the market in recent years, I'd be hard pressed to pick one over another, and I think the overall hue is more important than the actual pattern. When hunting at Sand Lake National Wildlife Refuge in South Dakota, I had all kinds of camouflage clothes, but they were all too dark and left me starkly silhouetted in the tan-colored cattails and marsh grass. I met another hunter who was wearing light tan work coveralls, and he blended in great. I saw him kill a deer, so I know the deer didn't see him. Try to pick clothes that blend with the foliage where you're hunting. In dark, shadowed timber, wear brown, dark green, and black clothing. On the desert or the prairie, wear tan and light green. On snow, wear white camo.

Skin

It doesn't make sense to me to select the perfect clothing color and do nothing with your face and hands. They stand out more than any other feature. Some hunters wear no face camouflage and still kill animals. Personally, I need every advantage I can get, and camouflage on my face gives me confidence. Fully camouflaged, I know an animal won't immediately spot my white mug hanging out. Probably the best face camouflage is a head net, and if you don't mind wearing one, that's the way to go. But I don't like face masks or head nets because they obstruct my vision and steam up my glasses. I prefer to paint my face with Chameleon Camouflage or similar products. It's more convenient.

Hands may be the most visible part of your body during a shot because they must move as you pull your bow, and movement is what catches an animal's eye. They should be camouflaged for that reason. The wool glove liners mentioned above are excellent camouflage. For hot weather, some companies make lightweight net gloves. Or you can simply use camouflage paint on your hands.

Hunting Pack

I consider a hunting pack a necessity. It not only contains items necessary for hunting, but it holds comfort and survival gear that allows you to hunt

Camouflage with a white background can be deadly on snow.

When hunting far off-road, many hunters prefer a larger pack like this with a small frame to support the weight. You can stuff enough gear in a pack like this to stay out several days. The bags on this pack are made of PolarFleece for silence.

long and hard, knowing you can survive the worst of conditions. A pack not only takes care of your needs, it gives you confidence.

Fanny packs, worn on a belt around your waist, are convenient and hold enough gear for short trips, but if you're hunting far off the road, you'll probably want something bigger. Many hunters use rucksacks, frameless bags with shoulder straps. Rucksacks are okay, but they'll tire your shoulders during a long day if filled with much weight. A better solution is a small pack with a frame of some kind that places the weight of the pack on your hips. I've used one like this for several years and have found it ideal—it doesn't interfere with shooting and it's strong enough for packing as much as a quarter of an elk.

At one time all packs were made of nylon, which is rugged but is also noisy. Now, dozens of companies produce fleece packs, which I recommend. Finally, a pack must be comfortable and reasonably light, or you'll avoid carrying it when you really need it. Select your items judiciously to keep the pack comfortably light. You must be able to hunt and shoot while wearing your pack.

What you carry in a pack depends on hunting conditions and on your personal preferences. I usually carry the following items in my pack: small flashlight with extra batteries and a spare bulb; map and compass; fire starter; knife and sharpener; small folding saw; first-aid kit; fifty feet of nylon cord; whistle for signaling; signal mirror; fluorescent plastic flagging; rain gear; bota bag full of water; toilet paper; lunch; bow-repair equipment (extra bow string, spare arrow rest, Allen wrenches for various parts on bow); camera and film; hunting license and tags; and game bags.

Binoculars and Scopes

No matter where you hunt, whether in deep woods or the open desert, you'll see more and hunt better with good optics.

Binoculars

Keep two things in mind when choosing binoculars — quality and size. Binoculars in the mid to high price range will give you best service in the long run. If you're just looking for a bargain (under $100) at the local

These rubber-armored Zeiss *(left)* and Swarovski 8 x 30 binoculars are excellent for hunting from timber to desert.

discount store, you're literally buying yourself one big headache. Cheap binoculars have poor glass and coatings, and they're often poorly aligned, which will give you a headache to end all headaches.

Buy full-sized binoculars. Mini-binoculars were the rage for a while, especially among bowhunters, but tiny glasses have some major drawbacks. Their worst fault is poor light-gathering ability. Increased brightness should be one of the benefits of binoculars.

Binoculars have a two-number designation, for example, 7 x 35 or 8 x 42. The first number refers to magnification, the second to the size of the objective (front) lenses. A 7 x 35 has seven-power magnification and 35mm objective lenses. No matter how high the quality of a pair of binoculars, small objective lenses will dim a scene rather than make it brighter. The bigger the objective lenses, the brighter the binoculars. For acceptable brightness, buy binoculars with at least 30mm objective lenses.

If you hunt mostly in deep woods, brightness is more important than high magnification. For such use, I recommend binoculars in the 5x to 7x range, such as Steiner's 6 x 30G, Ranging's 5 x 32 low-light binoculars, the Swarovski 7 x 30 compact, or any of the popular 7 x 35 models. These glasses give ample magnification for confined quarters, they're easy to hand hold because of the modest magnification, and they're very bright.

If you hunt deep woods and open areas, consider binoculars in the 7x to 8x range, a good all-around compromise. The most popular style is the 7 x 35, probably because it has adequate magnification while being easy to hand hold and bright enough for most uses. My favorite is the Bausch & Lomb 7 x 35 classic, but all good binocular manufacturers make 7 x 35s. You can get 8x binoculars from 8 x 30 to 8 x 42. Any quality binoculars in this range are suitable for all-around hunting.

If you hunt primarily in open country — desert, prairie, or alpine — then 9x or 10x would be most suitable. I know a lot of serious western hunters, and by far the most popular binoculars among them are the Zeiss 10 x 40s. For dollar value, the Bausch & Lomb Custom 10 x 40 is hard to beat.

If you wear eyeglasses, insist on binoculars with an eye relief long enough that you can wear your glasses and still get the full field of view through the binoculars. Some manufacturers list eye relief length in their literature. It should be at least 17mm for use with glasses. If the literature doesn't specify the length of the eye relief, call the company and ask.

Scopes and Big Binoculars

For ultra-long ranges, standard binoculars aren't enough. On many western ranges, you could view deer three or four miles away or farther, and a

In some areas, where visibility may be three or four miles, a spotting scope of 20x to 30x can save you a lot of walking. A scope must be mounted on a tripod.

scope of 20x to 25x is often needed just to see animals that far away, let alone judge them for quality. I don't recommend scopes over 30x because heat-wave distortion is so great that even on cool days, you can't see clearly with them. A zoom scope of 10x–30x or 15x–45x can be useful for viewing at varied distances. Any scope must be mounted on a tripod; you can't hand hold a scope steady enough to see well.

One problem with a scope is that you use only one eye, and the result can be eye strain. Big binoculars of 15x are more comfortable for long-term spotting. Steiner 15 x 80s and Zeiss 15 x 60s are two of the more popular versions. These are the ultimate for serious western game spotting. The major drawback is weight. They're too heavy for backpacking, and binoculars of this size must be used on a tripod.

Scents

Human Odor Eliminators and Cover-ups

Without question, your biggest obstacle as a bowhunter is your own body odor. Most big game animals use three senses to detect danger—sight, hearing, and smell — but their noses are their primary defense. An animal might see or hear you and not spook right away, but he only has to smell you once to know instantly you're bad news. That's why body odor is such a problem.

Cover-ups, ranging from fox urine to skunk scent to vanilla-based scents that smell like nothing in particular, have been around for years. Some hunters swear by them. Other hunters stand in the smoke of their campfires, figuring the smoke will mask their odor. The idea behind all cover-ups is that a strong natural, non-human aroma will mask your odor.

A new twist on this age-old idea is the human-scent neutralizer. The first in this line was Scent Shield, and a number of similar products have followed. These products chemically interact with human odor to neutralize it. These have been some of the hottest products to hit the hunting market in recent years.

Finally, many hunters wash their clothes and their bodies in baking soda or with unscented soaps and use powerful deodorants to reduce body odor. Many also seal their hunting clothes in plastic bags with pine boughs, sagebrush, or other native vegetation to mask what little body odor they couldn't wash away.

I'm not convinced any of these is a panacea for body odor, but these remedies help to some extent, particularly to avoid polluting a hunting area with strong body odor. After a few days without a bath, I've had mule deer smell me at distances farther than half a mile. Had I been able to wash regularly and reduce body odor, those deer probably wouldn't have smelled me that far away. But they would have at some point. At bow-shooting distances, animals can smell you no matter what you do.

The value of scent-reducing procedures, of course, depends on your style of hunting. If you simply walk 100 yards and climb into a tree stand, you can effectively reduce body odor to the point where animals will probably have a hard time smelling you. But what about when you're hiking the backcountry day after day, and have no really good way to wash your clothes or take a bath? In those circumstances, I question whether any procedure will solve your body-odor problem.

On a Roosevelt elk hunt in Oregon, Larry Jones and I diligently descented in every way possible, and elk still smelled us. After a few such experiences, Larry summarized our feelings about human odor and animals: "This stuff must really work. If you use this deodorant and spray down with this scent neutralizer and douse yourself with cover-up scent, and then keep the wind in your favor, those animals won't smell you." I agree. If you hunt into the wind so it's blowing from the animal to you rather than from you to the animal, the animal won't smell you. That's your only guarantee.

Attractor Scents

Attractor scents run the gamut from food aromas to estrus scents to pure urine. Probably the most commonly used attractors are doe-in-heat attractors. Manufacturers say these are made with urine taken from does during their estrus cycles. Similar products are available for elk, bears, and other animals.

I've talked to many whitetail hunters who've had success with attractors. Jim Martin of Independence, Missouri, who killed the Missouri state-record nontypical whitetail and other good bucks, uses a doe-in-heat scent (Indian Buck Lure) successfully in conjunction with mock scrapes. Sometimes he even lays a trail to his stand by putting these scents on his boots and has had bucks trail him right to his stand tree.

Some hunters swear by bear and elk lures and attractor scents for other animals.

Rob Kaufhold of Lancaster, Pennsylvania, said, "Once I start seeing scrapes in October, I use Bob Kirschner's Trailmaker. I put it on my boots to lay a trail to my stand, and I've had three deer, two bucks and a doe, follow my footsteps right to the tree." Noel Feather, famous for rattling, puts scents on cotton in film canisters and places these around his stand to pull deer into good shooting position as he rattles. He swears by them.

Some hunters report good success on other animals, too. In New Mexico, baiting bears is illegal, but Larry Sellers, a local hunter, has found an alternative—he uses sow-in-heat scent. He scouts extensively, and where he finds fresh sign, he saturates a log or soft earth with the scent and waits in a nearby tree stand. He's taken two bears that scored high on the Pope and Young scale this way.

Another hunter told me he thought scents should be outlawed for elk. "I put out cow-in-heat scent and a bull just went crazy. He wouldn't leave, and he paid no attention to me. That stuff should be illegal."

There's no question, then, that scents can help when used correctly. But don't expect miracles from them. I've used cow-in-heat scent for elk many times over a period of years. During those years, I've taken several bulls, but I don't think the scent played any part in my taking an animal. I've never seen a bull react positively to scent.

Rob Kaufhold said, "I've seen bad reactions to some lures. It seems they vary from batch to batch, or maybe they're old and have a strong ammonia smell. I've seen deer smell some scents and head for the hills."

Mike Dickess, an Ohio hunter who has killed many whitetails big enough to make the Pope and Young record book, said, "I killed one nice buck with a rut lure, but for every one like that, I could name dozens of times deer reacted badly to attractors, so I generally don't use them."

Russ Thornberry, a well-known whitetail hunter and writer, said, "In the name of science, I've tried every type of scent, but I have no evidence that they work. In Alabama, I put doe-in-heat lure on cloths and hung them in branches, and the smell scared the dickens out of everything that walked by. I've seen no response to scents but fear."

If the right scent is used in the right way, it could probably help your cause. Experiment. If you see positive results, keep using it; if you see negative reactions, quit. Keep in mind that scents offer no guarantees. Like all other products, they're no substitute for smart hunting.

9

Physical Conditioning

At one time I put all my emphasis on physical conditioning. I ran many miles, swam, and lifted weights to get ready for hunting, thinking that if I could just hunt far enough and long enough, I had to be successful. It didn't work. Physical conditioning alone wasn't enough. I've since learned that hunting knowledge and skill are more important. Nevertheless, physical conditioning is fundamental to good hunting. Good conditioning doesn't guarantee success, but bad conditioning can prevent it.

Physical Condition and Hunting Success

You don't have to be in great shape to walk 100 yards and climb into a tree stand, and if that's the only way you hunt, physical fitness may be irrelevant. But if you hunt on foot, and particularly in the West with its high elevations and steep grades, being in good shape means good hunting. I've asked several western mule-deer and elk guides why clients fail to take animals, and the most common reason they cite is poor physical condition. Either the clients couldn't get to the animals in the first place, or they were too exhausted to perform by the time they did and botched their chances.

Many of those clients were rifle hunters, but the effects may be even more severe for bowhunters. I've heard about rifle hunters who missed easy shots because they were breathing so hard they couldn't hold their sights on target. In bowhunting, I suspect many missed shots could be traced to the same problem. The better shape you're in, the better you'll withstand the strain of hunting, and the better you'll shoot in stressful situations.

Any endurance training, such as riding a stationary bike, improves overall conditioning and leg strength for better hunting performance and more accurate shooting.

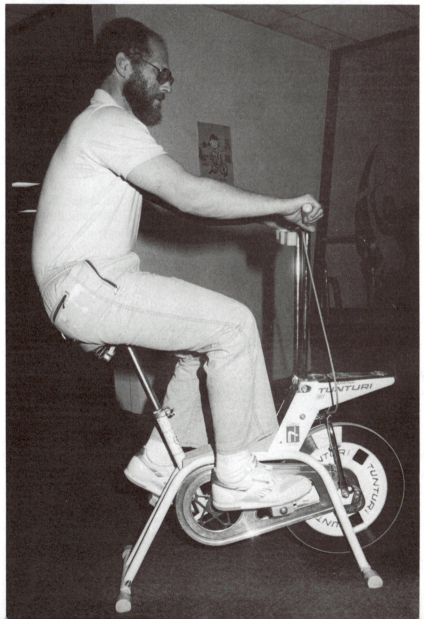

Physical condition not only affects overall hunting performance; it affects shooting ability, too. Prior to the 1984 Olympics, seventy-nine top archers went through eighteen months of intensive testing and evaluation to help researchers relate physical and psychological traits to tournament success. You can't directly apply all aspects of tournament archery to hunting, but they're similar in many respects. The results of these tests can be useful to bowhunters. One thing researchers found was that the major variable in archery success is leg strength. Archers with the strongest legs had the highest average scores. When you think about it, the logic is obvious. Shooting accuracy depends on stability, and strong legs provide that stability. If you're swaying like a cattail in the wind, your sights will be all over the target. Strong legs give your upper body a firm foundation.

Researchers also found a close correlation between a hunter's percentage of body fat and archery success. Archers with lower percentages of body fat had higher average scores than archers with higher percentages of body fat. This probably occurred because percent of body fat is strongly correlated with physical condition — the less fat, the better overall physical condition. Well-conditioned muscles provide the stability and endurance needed for accuracy under strenuous conditions.

Endurance Training

Endurance training is often called "aerobic" training, which means "with oxygen." It involves exercise you can maintain over a long period of time without running out of breath. Walking, running, swimming, cycling, jumping rope, and cross-country skiing are common endurance exercises. These produce a strong heart and lungs, reduce body fat, and build overall muscle tone, all valuable qualities for efficient bowhunting and accurate shooting.

Most doctors and physiologists recommend a complete physical examination before beginning any exercise program, particularly if you're over thirty-five and have not been training, or regardless of age if you have a family history of heart disease. The exam should include a stress electrocardiogram (in which your heart is monitored as you walk or run on a treadmill), because heart problems that might be unnoticed at rest will show up under stress.

The exercises you choose should emphasize the use of large muscle groups — thighs, chest, and shoulders — and particularly legs, for increased leg strength. They also must be exercises you can sustain over a long period without running out of breath. Nonstop activities like walking, running, swimming, and cycling yield benefits more quickly than stop-and-go sports like basketball and handball. A mix of sports might be best, because each works different muscles to build overall physical fitness. Once you've chosen suitable exercises, base your overall program on four variables: intensity, duration, frequency, and progression.

Intensity

To improve physical fitness, you must train at an intensity that will yield a desirable heart rate. Some physiologists use a formula to determine maximum heart rate—220 minus age. Thus, if you're twenty years old, your maximum rate is 200 (220 − 20 = 200). If you're forty years old, it's 180. If you're in poor condition, you should start at 70 percent of maximum heart rate, and if you're in good shape, you should train at about 80 percent. If you're forty and in reasonably good shape, your training heart rate would be about 144 beats per minute. That is, 180 (maximum heart rate) x .80 = 144.

To calculate heart rate, exercise long enough to make your heart beat quickly, and then stop and take your pulse for six seconds and multiply by ten to calculate the beats per minute. If your heart rate is slower than the prescribed training rate, work harder; if it's faster, slow down. If you're in poor shape, you might reach the training heart rate simply by walking; if you're in good shape, you might have to run hard to reach it.

Duration

An exercise must be maintained for at least twelve to fifteen minutes to be of major aerobic benefit. The longer the duration, the greater the benefit, although the returns diminish past a certain point. In a report on physical fitness for top archers, Rick McKinney, a world champion and Olympic medalist, said training for fifteen minutes increases physical condition roughly 8 percent, thirty minutes 16 percent, and forty-five minutes, about 17 percent.

"Since there is a major difference in conditioning gain between fifteen and thirty minutes and a minor difference between thirty and forty-five minutes, your best bet would be thirty minutes," McKinney wrote.

When you first start out, you may not be able to sustain an activity for thirty minutes, so begin exercising for twelve to fifteen minutes at a time, with a goal of working up to thirty minutes at a stretch.

Frequency

To maintain a good level of fitness, you also must exercise at least three non-consecutive days a week. Four or five would be better. If you lay off more than two days in a row, you begin to lose some of your conditioning. So plan to work out a minimum of three days a week, at least half an hour each time.

Progression

Walking is the most highly recommended exercise, especially if you're in poor shape. Once you get in shape, however, you won't be able to raise your heart rate to the training level by walking, so you should step things up by running, cycling, swimming, climbing hills, or carrying a pack with weight in it. You should progress gradually, starting at a comfortable and safe level, rather than trying to conquer the world in one day. With consistent effort over a couple of months, you'll attain great hunting condition. An excellent general training guide for overall fitness is *The Aerobics Program for Total Well-Being* by Dr. Kenneth Cooper.

Strength Training

In addition to aerobic training, which builds strength and overall condition, strength training of specific muscle groups can be helpful. Rick McKinney and Shari Rhoades developed a weight-training program for competitive archers. McKinney said the program is designed to strengthen muscles used in shooting, but it's well balanced to promote all-around condition.

"When I started training this way, I found right off I could hold my bow longer and remain steady," McKinney said. "There's no question it improved my stability. My scores jumped almost twenty points, and I set a world record about four months after I started this training program."

As a hunting archer, you'll reap similar benefits. The strength you gain will not only improve your stability and accuracy, it will help prevent injuries. Overuse injuries to the shoulders and elbows are common among bowhunters, and exercise will help prevent these. Exercises can be done either with free weights or on machines like the Universal Gym.

McKinney suggested, as a rule of thumb, that men start with half their body weight for leg exercises and one-fourth for arms and shoulders. Women should start with two-fifths of body weight for legs and one-fifth for arms and shoulders.

The two important terms involved in lifting are "repetitions" and "sets." A repetition is the number of times you lift a weight, and a set is the number of groups of repetitions. For example, if you lift a weight ten times and then stop, that's one set of ten repetitions. As a good starting point, do one set of ten to fifteen reps. After the third workout, do two sets, and after the eighth workout, increase to three sets. When you can do three sets and feel you could do several more, increase the weight five to ten pounds.

Some exercises that can improve your strength for bowhunting are squats, lunges, sit-ups, shoulder presses, lateral arm raises, and upright rowing.

Squats build strong thighs and buttocks. You can do these with barbells or on various machines. Stand straight with your feet at shoulder width, weight bar balanced on your shoulders. Squat until your thighs are nearly parallel with the floor, then stand back up. To prevent injury, keep your back straight and your head up.

Lunges develop strength and flexibility in the hamstrings and buttocks. Do them with a dumbbell in each hand or with a barbell on your shoulders. Stand straight and then lunge ahead with your left foot, keeping your right leg as straight as possible. Then thrust hard with the left leg to push yourself back to a standing position. Now lunge forward with the right leg, keeping your left leg straight, and thrust yourself back to a standing position. Keep your back straight and your head up throughout this exercise.

Sit-ups strengthen the stomach, which helps support the back. Lie on your back, hands locked behind your head and knees bent, and slowly curl to a sitting position. Don't jerk yourself up. Lower yourself slowly back to the floor.

The shoulder press strengthens your shoulders, upper back, and chest. Stand straight, holding a barbell at shoulder level, hands about six inches wider than shoulders, thumbs turned in toward each other. Push the bar up until your elbows lock. Lower the bar behind your head onto your shoulders, push it back up, and lower it to your chest. Repeat this alternating sequence. Keep your back straight.

Lateral arm raises strengthen the shoulders and upper back, which will help you pull and hold a bow steady. Use dumbbells or similar weights. Hold a weight in each hand and stand with your arms at your sides, palms in. Slowly lift your hands to shoulder level and lower them to your sides. Do bent-over lateral arm raises similarly, but bend at the waist with your upper body parallel to the floor. Hold the dumbbells hanging in front of you with palms facing in, and raise your arms sideways as high as possible. Lower them slowly.

Upright rowing strengthens the upper back, shoulders, biceps, and forearms. Stand with your feet at shoulder width, and hold a barbell in front of you, hands about six inches apart, thumbs toward body (you can do this with a dumbbell in each hand, too). Pull the bar to your chin, keeping your elbows higher than your wrists. Lower slowly and repeat.

10

Basic Hunting Methods

Hunting methods must meet certain requirements to be effective. Above all, they must allow you to see deer before they see you. Your method must also provide close-range shots, preferably at undisturbed, calm animals. The four hunting methods included in this chapter — stand hunting, stalking, calling, and still hunting — are the ones I consider best suited to bowhunting.

Stand Hunting

Statistics from the Pope and Young Club, the official records keeper for bowhunting trophies, show that 80 percent of all whitetails entered in the record book are taken by tree-stand hunters. About 70 percent of bears are taken over bait, which means the hunters used stands. Nearly 60 percent of all pronghorns are taken by hunters in blinds.

Stands work so well because you're sitting still while animals move toward you, the perfect scenario for seeing but remaining unseen. Stand hunting also gives you time to size up animals and make good shots. Jay Scott, a Colorado outfitter who uses tree stands for hunting mule deer, said, "The quality of shots from stands is far superior to stalking. Shooting distances are fifteen feet to thirty-five yards, and you can measure distances ahead of time with a rangefinder. Also, you have time to relax, to

Stand hunting depends largely on scouting. Look for fresh trails and other places of concentrated activity.

get yourself together. Deer don't know you're there, and you have a better chance for a clean kill. Also, you don't push the game around. You can hunt the same deer day after day."

Another advantage of stand hunting is that you reduce your chances of being smelled. When you are in a tree stand, your scent drifts some distance and dissipates before reaching the ground.

Any focal point of animal activity is a good place for a stand. In dry country, waterhole blinds can produce antelope and other big game.

Stand Sites

Any situation that funnels deer to a particular spot makes a likely location for a stand. The most obvious sites are trails that lead from bedding to feeding areas, particularly trail junctions. Fence crossings can be great places for stands, too. Jay Scott said, "We place stands where elk have knocked down fences or pushed down the top strands. Deer can jump any fence, but they'll walk 100 yards to easier spots. Also, they'll cross in cover. So we look for these strategic places and put stands there."

Some whitetail hunters pull the top two strands of barbed-wire fences together (with the landowner's permission) to create low, easy deer crossings that act as funnels. Antelope rarely jump fences, but they go under, and any point where the bottom strand is higher than normal is a likely crossing and a good place for a stand.

Rutting areas are naturals for stand sites during the rut — the breeding season. Active scrapes may be the best stand locations of all for whitetails. Scrapes are places where bucks paw the ground bare and leave their scent to attract does. Many elk hunters rely on stands near fresh wallows — places where bulls roll in the mud as part of the rutting ritual — for taking bulls each year.

Food sources are also good stand sites. In early fall, apple orchards and oak groves pull lots of deer. "I hunt deer at food sources, mostly white oaks and black oaks close to brushy, grown-over clearcuts where they bed," said Ohio hunter Mike Dickess. "I hunt all season, but even during the rut, I still hunt the food sources at the edges of clearcuts."

After the rut, whitetails' thoughts turn from mating to eating, and after about December 1, most serious hunters switch from hunting scrapes to food sources. Myles Keller said, "If I find a good food source, like an unpicked corn or soybean field, that's where I'll hunt."

Water can be the surest stand site of all under the right conditions, meaning dry country with limited water. Waterhole stands are deadly for mule deer, elk, and antelope in regions with limited water. Mineral licks also concentrate animals and make good stand sites.

Stand-hunting Principles

Four essential factors for every successful stand hunt are wind direction, visibility and clearance, undetected entrance and exit, and comfort. Your number one concern when stand hunting should be wind direction. Always place stands downwind of the game you plan to hunt. This requires some knowledge of the country and wind patterns. Several stand sites may be needed, so you should choose the best position for each wind direction.

The whole idea of hunting from a stand is to see animals before they see you and to get a clear shot. Study a location well before placing your stand. If necessary, do some clearing and pruning to ensure clear shots in several directions.

You have to be able to reach your blind without being seen, heard, or smelled by your quarry. Plan your setup so you can get into and out of your stand without detection. In many cases, particularly in the open as in antelope hunting, your only recourse is to reach your blind in the dark.

Some whitetail hunters actually use a rake to clear trails to their stands so they can come and go quietly.

A final but important consideration for stand hunters is comfort. Time equals success in stand hunting, and to devote the required time, you

Portable tree stands give you the flexibility to move quickly and fine-tune your location. This Vantage-Point tree stand hangs on a metal spike screwed into the tree. Always wear a safety belt.

must be comfortable. Have a good seat, and build your blind so you can move to stretch without being seen or heard. Proper clothing is important for comfort, too. In hot weather, wear cool, bug-proof clothes. In cold weather, dress in layers, starting with long johns. Add a light shirt, then a wool shirt, and top it off with a fleece or wool jacket. On your feet, wear felt-insulated pacs or "Mickey Mouse" boots, which have dead-air insulation.

Tree Stands

Tree stands can be either permanent or portable. If you hunt the same places year after year on private land, permanent stands are a good choice, but it's illegal to build permanent stands on public land in many states. Even if you can build a permanent stand, someone else might use it. Also, a permanent stand allows no flexibility. Unless you build several, you can't move to adapt to changing conditions. Most hunters use portable stands for those reasons.

Mike Dickess said, "I try to stay mobile, so I have several trees picked out. That way, if the wind isn't just right or the buck I want isn't coming close enough, I'll fine-tune my location. I've moved as many as four times in a fifty-yard circle. That's why I use portable stands."

Climbing stands, which attach around a tree with a bracket and help you shinny up rather than using tree steps, are great if your area has straight, limbless trees. I prefer climbers where they're feasible. Using a climbing stand requires a fair amount of strength, especially if you climb by "bear hugging" the tree and pulling yourself up. Some stands have hand climbers that double as seats to make climbing easier.

Some hunters prefer non-climbing stands that cinch tight to the tree with a rope or chain. With the Vantage Point tree stand, you screw a metal spike into the tree and hang the stand on the spike. This system works well because you can put spikes in selected trees and hang the stand up where you want it at the moment. (In some areas, it's illegal to screw or pound any object into trees. Check the laws before you go.)

Ladder stands are the simplest and quickest portables. You simply lean a ladder stand against a tree, secure it, and climb up. The major drawback is the bulk and weight of the stand and the limited height. In Texas, tripod stands are used in brush country where there are no trees to support tree stands. Jay Scott has used these Texas stands with good success while hunting mule deer in the oak brush of Colorado.

My personal preference for stand height is about fifteen feet, and many hunters seem to think that's about right. Rob Kaufhold said, "I don't like my stands more than fifteen to eighteen feet high, because if you're too high, you end up shooting straight down, which isn't the best shooting angle." Mike Dickess, on the other hand, said, "I'm big on getting high, and most of my stands are twenty-two to twenty-eight feet high. That gets you up where the deer are less likely to smell and see you."

Most serious tree-stand hunters scout ahead of the season to locate good trees and then prune limbs to clear shooting lanes. On private land, where other hunters won't find his stands, Kaufhold cuts lanes like spokes so he can shoot in all directions. "The deer sometimes use those shooting lanes as trails, which brings them right to my stand," Kaufhold said. "On private land, I also rake a path to my stand, so I can sneak in silently an hour before first light without using a light."

Before any hunt, check the bolts and connections on your stand to make sure there are no squeaks. Any slight noise as you move could spook an animal at close range. Many hunters carpet their stands for added silence. Jay Scott, an outfitter in Colorado, has all his hunters wear Bears Feet, padded boot covers made of PolarFleece, to eliminate foot noise.

The time of day should also be considered when planning your hunt. Pope and Young statistics show that about 50 percent of all whitetails are killed between 4 P.M. and sunset. The other peak period is from sunrise to about 10 A.M., when another 35 percent are taken. Obviously, if your time is limited, these are the periods to focus on. But if you have time to hunt longer, you probably should stay in your stand all day. Bucks, particularly during the rut, will move all day long, especially back in the brush where they're concealed.

Safety should be of primary concern to every stand hunter. A recent Hunter Safety Coordinators report for one three-year period included sixty-two accidents in which hunters fell from trees. Of these, twenty were fatal. Many other hunters who fell from tree stands were paralyzed for life. Tree-stand accidents are the most serious danger you face as a bowhunter. Before using any tree stand, check screws, bolts, and other structural points and inspect your tree steps. To keep both hands free for climbing and to prevent falling on your bow, pull your bow up on a rope after you're securely in your stand. Also, always use a safety belt.

Stalking

In a strict sense, stalking means you locate animals from a distance and then sneak within range of them. Pope and Young records show that nearly 70 percent of record-book mule deer, 30 percent of antelope, 25 percent of elk, and 60 percent of moose were taken by stalking.

Hunting method is more a function of country than species. In this typical South Dakota whitetail country, you can spot whitetails at a distance and stalk them just as you would mule deer.

Stalking starts with spotting. Open country where you can see long distances is ideal, of course, but spotting is possible even in dense, broken areas. I've done well stalking whitetails and blacktails in brushy draws and river bottoms where visibility was no more than 100 yards. I just look for a place with a view of some good country and sit there and watch until I see a stalkable buck. (See chapter 8 for details on optical equipment.)

Now let's suppose you've spotted a buck you want. If you're spotting early in the morning, when deer are easiest to see, the buck is probably feeding and moving. If you can get to him quickly, you might want to go after him immediately. Your best chance on a moving deer is to get in front of him and ambush him as he moves toward you to feed. Watch long enough to anticipate his path, and circle around ahead of him.

If that's not possible, you're often better off waiting for him to bed. By mid-morning, deer usually have settled in for the day, and you have all day to work on them. Even after you've seen a buck bed, take your time. He may move, and you want to keep an eye on him until he's settled in for the day. You should also plan out a good stalking route. Study the terrain with your binoculars.

First, chart a feasible route to the deer. In some places that's easy, but in vertical or brushy country, just getting to a deer can be difficult. Then carefully study landmarks that mark the deer's location. Deer often lie where they're nearly invisible, and the toughest part of a stalk can be finding a buck once you get close. Take note of big trees, rocks, or bushes that will help mark the buck, and if you have a topographic map (which you should), make some notes on it.

Look for other animals, too. Spooking unseen deer is probably the single biggest reason for blown stalks, so try to locate fringe deer so you can avoid them.

Finally, analyze the wind. With binoculars, you often can watch grass or moss hanging from trees near your quarry to judge wind direction. If that doesn't work, make some assumptions based on what the wind is doing at your position. Normally, stalking is best soon after sunrise, when thermals are blowing steadily downhill, or from late morning through the afternoon, when they're blowing uphill. Probably the worst time is mid-morning, when thermals are switching.

If you've taken time to analyze and plan, the rest of a stalk will take care of itself for the most part. You should foil the deer's sense of smell, his most critical sense, with the wind. Your only remaining concerns are his sight and hearing, which can be minimized with the right clothes. (See chapter 8 for details.)

Close-range stalking depends on quiet footing. From left to right: Stocking feet for close work on noisy ground; lightweight canvas shoes with soft, rubber soles for all-around stalking; and Bears Feet boot covers to silence heavy boots.

You may have wondered how a white cat, in plain sight, can stalk and kill a bird on a bare lawn. The answer is simply slow movement. Ultimately, your stalking success will hinge on the same principle. Slow movement gets you close to the deer. Not only does the deer not notice your movement, but deliberate motion allows you to place your feet and hands carefully so you make virtually no sound.

As you get close to a buck, re-locating it can be difficult. Use your binoculars to look for an antler tine, a shining nose, or a flicking ear. Partners can help each other on hard-to-locate bucks. Avid mule deer hunter Greg Silva regularly hunts with his wife. They've worked out a system of hand signals, and they take turns guiding each other in on bedded bucks.

Using this approach, you can get within range of most bucks you see. You have to define your own range based on your shooting ability, but once you're within your effective shooting range, stop. If you try to get too close, you'll blow it.

"I used to always try for twenty yards, but now I think that's too close," Bill Krenz said. "At that distance, you can scarcely draw your bow. I think you're better off reaching your maximum effective range and stopping there. For me that's about forty yards. At that range, I'm a lot calmer than at twenty, and I can at least move to draw my bow without spooking the buck.

"Above all, I try to get a shot where the buck doesn't know I'm there. I've tried to get away from the old rifle mentality of kicking the deer out and blasting away. With a bow that's insane."

Calling

Calling includes any method in which you hide and try to bring animals to you by making some sort of sound. This method is well suited to bowhunting because, in essence, it's a form of stand hunting — you remain motionless and let animals come to you. I'll focus mostly on antler rattling here, but the same principles apply to all types of calling.

Antler rattling works particularly well for white-tailed and black-tailed deer. It's best during the rut, because it simulates the sound of bucks fighting over a doe. Most hunters agree the best time is the two weeks prior to the peak of the rut. In northern latitudes, that generally means the first two weeks in November.

"It drops off when does come into heat around November 20," said Sonny Templeton, a successful Montana hunter. "You have trouble pulling bucks away from hot does then. But after most of the does are bred, toward the end of November, it seems to pick up again. Bucks are still hot

Rattling has caught on as one of the best ways to call in deer, particularly whitetails and blacktails. Rattling on the ground can be effective, but you need good concealment. Don't be in a hurry to move, because bucks may sneak in slowly.

and bothered, and there aren't enough does to go around, so they'll investigate antler rattling then."

Antler rattling — or any type of calling, for that matter — can be approached in one of three ways. First, you can rattle blind. That is, you sneak through the woods quietly, blinding in periodically and rattling antlers. If nothing shows up within half an hour or so, you move to a new spot and try again. The problem with this approach is that you never know whether any bucks are within earshot, and they can sneak up on you easily. The second option is to locate bucks first, sneak close to them, and rattle the antlers. The third method is rattling from a tree stand, which gives you all the advantages of tree stand hunting. The drawback is that you're tied to one spot. But if you've done your homework, you know the bucks are there, and during the rut bucks are moving regularly. If you call from one spot long enough, a ripe buck eventually will come within earshot. Most serious hunters stay put for at least three to four hours, rattling occasionally during that period. To make this method work, put your stand in thick brush where bucks feel comfortable. They may not approach you out in the open.

I'm not convinced that the type of antlers you use makes a lot of difference. On one hunt I tried three different kinds—two styles of synthetics and a pair of old shed antlers that sounded woody. Bucks came to all three. Far more important, I think, is where you rattle (in a place with plenty of bucks, and a good blind) and how you rattle. A standard rattling sequence would be to clash and grind the antlers for a minute or so, wait thirty seconds to a minute and rattle for another half-minute. If you're on the ground, scratch the antlers in the ground and brush to sound like two bucks stomping and pushing each other around. As you rattle, always have an arrow nocked and your bow ready, because a buck may come on the run.

If nothing shows up right away, wait ten minutes or so and repeat the sequence, wait another ten minutes and repeat it again. If no bucks come in after thirty minutes, move on and try a new location. If you're in a tree stand, rattle every fifteen to thirty minutes for three or four hours. Have confidence and keep rattling. It doesn't work every time, but when it does, it's exciting.

Calling with a commercially made call can be combined with rattling or used independently. I've used a doe-bleat call successfully in conjunction with rattling. The grunt call may be even more effective. Many white-

Basic calling equipment includes rattling antlers (these are synthetic), a bleat call, and a grunt call. These can be used alone or in combination with each other.

tail hunters report better results with the grunt call than with rattling antlers. Rob Kaufhold is typical: "I've never had great success rattling, and I have seen negative reactions. Grunt calls, on the other hand, are fantastic. One time, I blew the call and a buck ran right up under my stand. Another time, I grunted and a buck came into view but stopped out of bow range. When I grunted again, he came right in. It's also good for pulling in deer you see passing out of range, seventy to eighty yards away, and for stopping animals for a better shot."

Still Hunting

The Reader's Digest *Great Encyclopedic Dictionary* defines "still" as (1) "making no sound, silent"; (2) "free from disturbance or agitation, peaceful, tranquil." These are the implied meanings in still hunting. You hunt on foot, moving slowly, making as little sound as possible, leaving the area free from disturbance. Still hunting differs from stalking in that you don't know exactly where animals are ahead of time. You move through the woods, spotting as you go.

Scouting is even more important in still hunting than in other hunting methods, because unless you know animals are close by, you'll soon lose the needed concentration. Shari Fraker, who still-hunts for elk, said, "Scouting means knowing where they are. After scouting, you don't blunder through the woods, hoping you'll see elk. You know you'll see them. Then hunting becomes a matter of expecting, not hoping." The same applies to deer and all other animals.

Still hunting is more than quiet walking; it's a very controlled art. To do it right, you take a step or two and then stand quietly, watching and listening. When you're sure you have seen and heard all there is to see or hear from that position, you slowly take another step or two and stop to watch and listen again. Slow movement is key. You're not out there to cover ground, but to see animals. In essence, still hunting is roving stand hunting. You move a short distance to get a new perspective and you take a stand. For best results, you should be standing far more than moving. I suggest moving one-quarter of the time and standing three-quarters.

Kneel frequently to look under branches and brush. A deer's body might be totally obscured by limbs, but his legs could be obvious underneath. And use your binoculars. In a maze of branches, your naked eye might never notice an antler tine or the tip of a tail, but binoculars isolate and magnify those details and make them stand out clearly. High magnification isn't as important as adequate brightness. Binoculars such as the Steiner 6 x 30G and Ranging 5 x 32 are well suited to still hunting in timber.

Hunt into the wind. Human scent eliminators and cover-ups might help, but don't count on them. Hunt into the wind, or at least crosswind. If the wind is swirling, you're better off not still hunting, because you'll spook animals needlessly.

If you really know your area and the animals there, you can still-hunt for bedded game during midday. But seeing a bedded deer in thick brush before he sees you is a tough assignment. You have a far better chance of seeing animals if they're up and moving. On normal days, the first and last hours of daylight are by far the best. On stormy days and during the rut, deer may move all day long, and you can do well still hunting throughout the day. I've done very well on both deer and elk at midday in a gentle rain or snow.

Cool conditions not only keep animals moving, but give you quiet footing. A light-to-medium, steady wind—just enough to cover your sounds and keep your scent from deer, but not strong enough to force them into cover—tops off the perfect day. If the woods are dry or crusted with snow, you would be better off calling or hunting from a stand.

11

Making the Shot

The idea of bowhunting isn't just to get "some shooting." Anyone can do that. A lot of things go into the making of a hunter and the enjoyment of hunting, but the bottom line is clean kills and meat on the table. A good hunter not only hunts well but makes killing shots, recovers his animals, and turns them into edible meat. Those are the steps covered here.

Shot Selection

Accuracy

You are likely to hear experienced bowhunters talk about the importance of the right kind of broadheads, heavy arrows, and heavy bow weights for killing animals cleanly. These are all important, but emphasizing these clouds the real issue—shot placement. It's often said an arrow kills by hemorrhage, and that's certainly true, but an animal hit in the heart or lungs dies almost instantly from organ failure, not from bleeding to death. If you put an arrow in the right spot, all other considerations are academic. Shot placement is the essence of game recovery, and that starts with accuracy. I've covered the basics of accuracy in earlier chapters, so I won't dwell on them here, except to say that making good hits is no accident. Work on the details of tackle selection, bow tuning, and shooting practice outlined in earlier chapters.

Distance

A friend of mine considers forty yards a long shot and adamantly insists no one should shoot beyond that distance. I, too, consider forty yards a long distance, but I'm not about to say that's the maximum shooting distance for all archers. Some archers can shoot accurately out to sixty yards or farther, and others can scarcely hit a bale of hay at thirty. You have to determine maximum shooting distance for yourself. Go about it semi-scientifically by putting up a deer target and shooting from various distances to see how far back you can get while still landing all your arrows in the vital organs (heart and lungs). Some hunters do this with a paper plate, because the plate is roughly the size of a deer's vital chest area. When you start missing, you're beyond your effective range.

Keep in mind, though, that this practice is done under ideal conditions. To learn your practical effective range, test yourself under bad conditions. Shoot in a hard wind, for example. Even if your "paper plate" accuracy is fifty yards on a calm day, it may shrink to twenty-five or less in a strong wind. Your effective distance may also be less in rain or snow, in

Simply getting close enough doesn't mean you have a good shot. You can't shoot through weeds, grass, or limbs. Wait until an animal presents an open shot.

bad visibility conditions, or when shooting up or down steep hills or in the brush. Deflections off branches and twigs are a major cause of missed shots or bad hits, so your effective range will be a lot shorter in the woods than in the open. Practice under all of these conditions, not only to develop your skill, but to learn your limitations.

Buck fever may also play a part in determining your effective range in the field. In a tree stand, you usually see a buck coming and have time to plan the shot and calm yourself. But on the ground, you're often surprised by an animal, and you're right at eye level. At ultra-close distances, your nerves can go to pieces. Steve Gorr, who guides antelope hunters each fall, said, "I've seen guys who shoot release aids and sights, deadly shots, miss a dozen shots at antelope less than twenty yards away and then make clean kills at fifty to seventy yards. Killing game under twenty yards has nothing to do with shooting ability. It's all between your ears." That's one reason for shooting from your maximum effective range rather than getting too close. You're calmer at a distance, and so are the animals.

An alert, tense animal can explode at the moment of the shot. Hunters call this "jumping the string." An animal can jump at the sound

This buck is close enough, but he presents a bad target because he's alert and set to jump the string. Try to get shots at calm, unaware animals.

of your bow going off (thus, the value of a quiet bow) or the sudden movement of the limbs. The potential for jumping the string is much greater with alert animals than with calm ones. So part of good shot placement is shooting at calm animals.

This brings us back to distance. At ultra-close ranges, an animal will notice the slightest movement and hear the slightest sound, even an arrow sliding across a rest. When it does, it will react much more violently than it would at longer distances. As Bill Krenz, an accomplished deer stalker, said, "The ideal range for me is twenty-five to thirty yards. But that's close enough. I used to try to get too close, like ten yards. Now I prefer to stay back because of the string-jumping potential. I want that buck calm. It's important to wait for just the right moment."

The point is, you need to strike a balance. Always try to get within your effective shooting range under the given conditions. But stop there. Don't try to get too close. Stay far enough away not to alert the animal. That's the key to getting good shots at calm animals.

Placement

One book on bowhunting for whitetails has an illustration showing only a buck's head and part of his neck above some grass. The caption reads: "A buck standing in tall cover offers little, but maybe you can punch an arrow through those weeds and into his neck."

That kind of advice makes me sick. The neck is nothing but bone, muscle, and gristle. Nobody in his right mind would purposely shoot for the neck. And anybody who's shot more than a dozen arrows in his life knows you can't "punch" an arrow through weeds or anything else. It takes only one tiny twig to throw an arrow off course. Just getting close doesn't mean you have a shot. Use restraint, and if you don't have a clear shot at the vitals of a deer, don't shoot.

The vitals are simply the lungs and the heart, the only places I'd recommend shooting big game. They present the largest vital area of an animal, so you have a little leeway in shot placement, and hitting one of these organs guarantees the surest, quickest kill. A deer or an elk shot through both lungs or the heart rarely goes farther than 100 yards, and I've seen many go less than 50.

At close range, you might actually shoot for the heart, but in most cases, the safest target is the lungs. To find the aiming point, first draw an imaginary line straight up from the front "elbow." Often you can see a very distinct vertical crease behind an animal's front leg, which makes a good indicator. Then draw an imaginary line horizontally through the deer's chest slightly below the midline. The place where the two lines meet marks the ideal aiming point. At that point, and several inches in each direction, your arrow will go through both lungs. If it's too far back, it will hit the liver. If this happens, the animal will bleed to death in a short period, and you'll recover him. If your arrow hits low, it will hit the heart, as good as a lung hit.

Be careful not to aim too high, because the tops of the lungs aren't nearly as blood rich as the lower lungs. Furthermore, you actually can shoot through an animal's chest just below the backbone and never recover the animal. Such an arrow would probably hit the lungs, but not squarely enough to collapse them. Because of the minimal blood flow there, the animal won't bleed to death. Therefore, I suggest aiming *below* the midline of the chest. If your arrow does hit a little high, it will still be a killing shot.

A broadside chest shot presents the best angle, although slightly quartering away is acceptable. Strongly quartering shots, however, are risky. Shari Fraker, an avid elk hunter and shot-placement expert, says, "At a strong angle, your arrow can deflect off ribs or tissue, and this problem is

This is the shot you want. To pick the best shooting point, imagine a horizontal line through the deer's body just below midline and a vertical line up from the elbow. Aim where the lines intersect.

Every animal has a distinct track, so study the tracks of the animal you're trailing so you recognize them instantly. You may not always have a good blood trail to follow.

compounded by shooting angle, either strongly quartering or up or down-hill. Compare it with skipping a rock on water. The greater the angle, the easier it is to skip the rock. It's the same with an arrow.

"That's why I say a broadside shot is best. You're playing the odds. On a scale of one to ten, you want to get as close to ten as possible, and that's what the broadside shot gives you. That's the best angle to collapse both lungs. From there, the score falls off until you get all the way to the rear or head on, which I'd give a minus ten."

Trailing

Even a well-hit animal can travel some distance. And, of course, you can't always guarantee a perfect hit. Eventually, if you hunt enough, you'll trail some game, which is part of bowhunting. Trailing must be perfected right along with shooting ability and hunting technique.

Follow up every shot. If you're in open country, run to the nearest vantage point and keep the animal in sight as long as possible. The easiest way to recover animals is to watch them go down, but, of course, that's not always possible. In some cases, you may not even know whether you hit an animal. If you aren't sure, go immediately to the point where the deer was standing and mark that place so you can find it again. Then look for your arrow. If you find it clean, you know you missed. If not, the arrow could tell you a lot about the hit. If you don't find the arrow, begin searching carefully for blood sign. If you don't find any blood, track the animal as far as possible. He could travel some distance, 100 yards or more, before any blood hits the ground.

If you find signs of a hit, you must decide whether to wait or to follow the animal immediately. If you're sure of a solid chest hit, or if you see foamy blood sprayed onto the ground, you know the deer was hit in the lungs and is already down. If you know you hit him in the chest, but aren't sure where, wait an hour or so. Even if he dies immediately, the meat won't spoil in that time, and you've lost nothing but a little time. If the animal doesn't die quickly, the longer you wait, the better your chances of recovery. A liver-hit animal, for example, will bleed to death in an hour, and you'll find him in his first bed. But if you push him, he could travel far enough to make recovery difficult.

If you know the animal was hit in the gut — either you saw the hit or find greenish juices on the arrow or on the ground — then back off. He will lie down soon, and that's where you must find him. If you startle him, he could travel several miles, leaving little or no blood trail, and your chances of finding him are zip. If you shot the animal in the morning, wait four to five hours before trailing. If you shot him in late afternoon, wait until the next morning to start trailing.

My friend Larry D. Jones taught me a cardinal rule of trailing: stick with the trail. That might seem obvious, and it's not hard to do when you find blood sprayed out by the pint, but sometimes the blood trail gets sparse, a drop or two of blood every ten feet. You may convince yourself the animal has quit bleeding, so you quit the trail to course ahead like a bird dog, hoping to find the animal or luck onto obvious sign.

Stick with the trail. On several occasions while hunting with Larry, I've gone on ahead, trying to anticipate an animal's route. While I did that, Larry patiently snooped around, looking for the trail. Time after time, he picked it up heading the opposite direction. I no longer put much credence in the theories that wounded animals head downhill or seek water or hole up in the nearest cover. Those are good last-resort guidelines, but before you try them, sleuth out the trail instead.

Following a major blood trail is easy. But even mortally wounded animals may leave a sparse trail, especially with a high chest hit that bleeds inside the body. That's when you learn trailing skills. If you just walk along, you'll miss hidden sign and swear the animal has quit bleeding, but if you get on your hands and knees, the trail will be obvious. Late one evening I shot an elk that covered a lot of ground quickly. Before long, darkness set in, and I had to trail with a flashlight. I couldn't see well in the dim beam, so I crawled and was amazed at how easily I detected pinhead spots of blood with my face close to the ground. You can trail very well in the beam of a flashlight (a gas lantern works even better), so don't give up just because of darkness. That's one reason your hunting pack should include a flashlight along with spare batteries and an extra bulb.

Crawling not only gives you a close-up view, but a better angle. Often, blood running down an animal's side or leg won't drip to the ground, but it will smear onto bushes and grass. You may never see this sign looking downward. But from a low angle looking up, you'll see blood smears on the underside of vegetation.

On a skimpy blood trail, you must rely on other signs, too. Overturned rocks, broken twigs, and mud smeared on rocks all indicate an animal's passing. Once, while trailing an elk, I lost the blood trail. Noticing several places where pine needles had been disturbed, I crawled along for half an hour and finally found a speck of blood, confirming that these were indeed the elk's tracks. I eventually recovered the elk.

Tracks, of course, are the surest sign next to blood. At the very start of a trail, study the animal's tracks for distinctive marks. Then they'll stand out surprisingly well as you follow the trail, even when they're mixed with other animals' tracks. Every animal has a distinctive stride length. When you find two clearly visible tracks made by your animal, use an arrow or a stick to measure the distance from one track to the next (a big buck might have a stride of twenty-four inches, a bull elk twenty-eight). Then use the arrow or stick as a tracking gauge. If you find one track but can't clearly see the next, lay one end of the gauge on the visible track and inspect the ground at the other end of the gauge. That's where the next track will be. I've tracked elk and deer several hundred yards across hard ground using this method.

If you simply can't follow the trail any longer, your last resort is to visually search for the animal. Try to anticipate where he might have gone and search systematically. Don't wander haphazardly. Mentally map out the area in quadrants, and then search back and forth to make sure you're not overlooking any possible cover. Keep looking until you've covered every base. If you've spent a full day, ten to twelve hours, searching for an animal and still can't find him or any fresh clues, then you've probably done all you can. But until that point, keep looking.

Meat Care

An old cartoon shows a kid sitting on the toilet with the caption, "A job isn't done until you've finished the paperwork." Similarly, the job of hunting isn't finished until your animal is wrapped in freezer paper. Only then can you say the job is finished. Allowing meat to spoil through neglect or ignorance is worse than losing a wounded animal.

From mid-October on, meat care isn't a major problem in northern latitudes, because fall weather will cool meat quickly. If you're hunting close to home, you can drag a deer out to your car and take it home for processing. But in the West, many bow seasons open in August, when the weather is too hot for quick meat cooling. Under these conditions, you can find yourself in the backcountry, where you can't get meat to a cooler for several days. In those situations, you must know how to handle an animal.

The key is to get body heat out of a carcass. It's not air temperature that spoils meat, but internal body heat. Hot weather keeps body heat from dissipating rapidly enough to prevent spoilage. Field-dressing (gutting) the animal is the first step.

To field-dress a deer, lay the animal on its back and slit the hide along the belly from chin to anus, being careful not to cut into the stomach or intestines. (If you plan to cape the deer for mounting, cut only from the brisket to the anus.) Cut the windpipe and esophagus at the chin and loosen them from the neck so they can be pulled into the body cavity. Next, cut around the anus to loosen it so the intestines can be pulled out through the body cavity. Reach into the body cavity and cut the diaphragm loose from the inside of the rib cage. Roll the deer onto its side and pull the viscera onto the ground. You may have to cut additional connective tissue loose inside to get everything out. Wipe the inside of the body cavity with a clean rag. If any internal organs have been punctured, contaminating the inside of the deer, wash the body cavity thoroughly with clean water and then wipe it dry.

Skinning

In cold weather, when temperatures drop to freezing or lower at night, skinning isn't really necessary. Besides, leaving the hide on prevents drying and helps keep the meat clean, which can be especially helpful in horsepacking and other backcountry situations where you can't handle the meat

Body heat is the major threat to meat in hot weather, so gut an animal quickly. Make sure you remove all organs, including the windpipe and esophagus all the way to the chin, and wipe the body cavity clean.

as carefully as you'd like. Leave the hide on until you take the animal to cold storage or to camp. There you can skin and bag it under clean conditions.

In hot weather — say with daytime temperatures higher than sixty degrees and nighttime temperatures no lower than forty — skinning pro-

To speed the cooling process, skin an animal on the spot. If you can't hang the deer, skin one side and lay out the skin as a drop cloth. Then roll the animal onto the clean hide and skin the other side.

motes the needed cooling and could save the meat. During hot, late-summer bow seasons, I suggest skinning an animal immediately in the field. While doing that, you need to bag the meat to keep it clean and to keep flies off. I recommend that you always carry lightweight cheesecloth game bags for that purpose when early-season hunting.

To promote cooling, hang the carcass in the shade or drape it over a log so air can circulate on all sides. Smaller animals such as deer and antelope will cool well this way, although it's a good idea to open up the hip and shoulder joints for quicker cooling. Big animals such as elk should be quartered; they cool very slowly otherwise. Bone sour, the result of slow

Any time you skin an animal in the field, bag the meat in a hurry to keep off dirt and flies. During early seasons, always have game bags and a packframe for packing the meat.

cooling, is particularly common in the hip joints and shoulders. To prevent that, slice down the insides of the back legs to open up the hip joints and cut under the front legs to open up a space between the legs and the chest.

Boning

If you have to pack animals a long way on your back, boning the meat (that is, removing all the bones) can reduce the weight you have to carry. Boning also enhances cooling. When boning an animal in the field, you must have game bags available to keep the meat clean.

Boning helps to reduce weight and speeds cooling. With the animal lying on its side, start by skinning the upper half of the animal from head to tail. Then cut off the front leg. (This is easy to do because it's held in place only by muscle.) Bag the leg to keep it clean.

Remove the back leg next. Start on the inside of the pelvis and work toward the back, slicing the meat cleanly from the pelvic bone. Soon you'll come to the hip joint. Push hard on the leg to break this joint open, and then continue to cut along the pelvis until the entire back leg comes loose. Bag the leg. To reduce weight further, you can later remove the bones from the front and back legs.

Finally, slice the meat off the ribs. Start at the brisket and work around the body to the backbone, much as you'd fillet a fish. Rib meat, flanks, backstrap, and neck come off in one big piece. You can cut this into two or three pieces to keep weight down.

When you've finished the top side, flip the carcass over and do the same on the other side. In hot weather, you must bag meat to keep off flies. Hang the meat in the shade, or if daytime temperatures are too hot, hang the meat at night and wrap it in sleeping bags during the day to keep it cool.

Preserving Meat

Meat processors say life begins at forty (forty degrees, that is), so if nighttime temperatures are dropping to forty degrees or lower, you can keep meat in the field for several days. The best way, especially if daytime temperatures are getting too warm, is to hang the meat at night without the game bags to cool it thoroughly. Then in the morning re-bag the meat, stack it on a clean tarp, and cover it with sleeping bags. With a good layer of bags, the meat temperature will rise no more than three to four degrees during the day. After sundown, hang it again for re-cooling. You can keep meat in the field for a week or more this way, even if daytime temperatures rise to sixty degrees or higher. This is also a good way to transport meat in your vehicle on a long drive home.

If you can't cool meat to forty degrees or lower at night, then you need to get it into cold storage within three days. If you're going into the backcountry, always line up packing services ahead of time, so you know you can get the meat out. If you follow these steps, you end up with great table fare, the sign of a successful hunter.

12

Deer

In a book covering only fundamentals, I can't write a complete profile on every big game species in North America. So here I'll sketch the most popular bowhunting animals. This chapter covers whitetails, mule deer, and blacktails, the three major deer species.

White-tailed Deer

Is it any wonder whitetails are the most popular game animals in America? Found in all of the contiguous forty-eight states (although not many live in Utah, Nevada, and California) and the eight Canadian provinces bordering the United States, whitetails are within reach of more hunters than any other big game. They're smart enough to be a challenge, but abundant enough to give everyone hope of bagging one. They're beautiful and good eating, essential qualities for a great game animal.

During the summer, bucks grow antlers and does nurse fawns. Since these activities require a large amount of energy, deer are active, feeding more than at any other period of the year.

Around the first week in September, bucks shed the velvet off their antlers and enter a sparring phase, when they carry on normal routines but also spar with each other to establish dominance. About October 15, the bucks start making scrapes and chasing does, in what biologists call the courtship phase of the rut. That lasts until about November 15, when does start coming into heat. The peak breeding period lasts from about November 15 through November 30. If a doe doesn't get bred the first time around, she will have secondary estrus cycles in December or later, so limited rutting may continue well into winter. This calendar holds for most northern whitetail ranges. In the South, the rut peaks a month or so later.

Scouting

Most serious whitetail hunters emphasize scouting, particularly in midsummer, July and August, when you can actually *see* whitetails. Stan Chiras has taken more than seventy whitetails from New York to Montana, and he starts scouting in July. First he studies maps and talks to landowners to locate potentially good areas, and then he visits those places and watches for deer in the evenings, using binoculars to judge trophy quality. "In summer, whitetails come out early in the evenings, and you can see them easily," he explained. "All I want to do in summer is find a good buck. He'll still be there in the fall."

Mike Dickess of Ironton, Ohio, said, "In August, bucks seem to come out of the woodwork, feeding in open fields where you can see them. One night in Ohio I saw ten bucks in one field. By the second week in September, they quit coming out. I try to locate a couple of good bucks early, and then I stick with them through the season."

Locating deer early points you toward good general locations, but it doesn't tell you exactly how or where to hunt. That's where on-the-ground scouting comes in. Within their home ranges, deer have key areas where they eat, bed, breed, and find security. In mid-fall, you should look for trails between these areas. In typically dense whitetail cover, trails are well defined, but even in more open country whitetails will follow certain paths. On Colorado's nearly treeless prairies, Dave Holt looks for bottlenecks where deer cut corners along winding creeks or follow steep banks or other obstacles. In big, open woods, deer seem to wander aimlessly, but even there, they prefer certain routes. John Mundinger, who studied whitetails in the rolling, dense forests near Swan Lake, Montana, found that whitetails traveled along ridge tops, the bottoms of draws, and around the margins of potholes and small marshes.

About October 15, rut sign starts showing up. Rub trees, where bucks have thrashed trees in mock battle, may not tell you exactly where to hunt, but they indicate buck numbers and size. Most hunters agree — the bigger the rub trees, the bigger the bucks. Rubs on trees over four inches in diameter probably were made by large bucks.

Scrapes, places where a buck paws the ground to clear away debris, are the rut sign most hunters look for most seriously. While making a scrape, the buck urinates on glands inside his back legs and rubs the glands together. Urine dropping from the glands leaves the buck's scent on the scrape. Normally, the buck reaches up and pulls at a twig with his mouth to leave scent on the branch from glands on his head. In most cases, you'll find scrapes under overhanging branches, with broken twigs hanging down. Scrapes are signposts for does looking for suitable mates.

Not all scrapes necessarily mark great stand locations, but like rub trees, the abundance of scrapes suggests the number of bucks present.

Even where trees are scarce, rutting whitetail bucks will rub on something. In South Dakota, cedar fence posts will do nicely.

Secondary scrapes are made quickly and may not be revisited. But as the breeding period nears, certain scrapes will be used over and over. These primary scrapes become hubs of activity, and they indicate good stand locations.

Winter scouting can be helpful for the following season, because, barring major land or weather changes, deer will follow the same patterns from year to year. Many hunters look for shed antlers in winter as indicators of how many bucks survived the hunting season.

Many also consider winter the best time to analyze sign. Bob Fratzke, a well-known hunter from Minnesota, said, "In winter when the trees and bushes are bare, I'll see scrapes, rub lines, and trails I didn't know existed. I'm just looking and analyzing. I look for stand trees, too. With trees bare, that's the best time to pick your stand trees. You can get a good idea whether there will be adequate cover late next fall. I always carry a pole saw in spring and cut branches that could be in the way for shooting. I've got lots of trees cleaned out — lots — because I move around during the season."

Effective Hunting Methods

As mentioned in chapter 10, about 80 percent of record-book whitetails are taken from tree stands. That's true mostly because of the nature of whitetails. They are reasonably habitual, using the same trails regularly, returning to their rutting grounds day after day. Even whitetail country lends itself to stands, because it has plenty of trees in the right places. There are exceptions, as on the prairies or in brush country, but generally speaking, your best chance for bagging a whitetail is from a tree stand, if you have the patience to hunt this way. Use your knowledge of trails, rutting grounds, food sources, and so forth, gained by scouting, as a guide to stand location (for details on stand hunting, see chapter 10).

Still hunting is the second-most-common method listed by Pope and Young for whitetails, although only about 5 percent of the whitetails reported were taken this way. A mystique has grown up around whitetails that almost implies these deer can't be taken by a hunter on foot. In most cases, odds are against it, but whitetails are flesh and blood like any other deer, and under the right conditions, they can be had by hunters on foot.

Of course, the key phrase there is "under the right conditions." For whitetails, that means fairly high deer numbers, reasonably open cover so you can move quietly and see fairly well, and quiet footing (for details, see still hunting in chapter 10). When conditions are right, I prefer still hunting to stand hunting, and I've taken several whitetail bucks while doing it.

Calling is one of the best techniques for whitetails because they're vocal animals that respond well to calls. Moreover, hunting seasons in many states take place during the rut when bucks are most responsive. Whitetails make a number of varied sounds, and if you want to get scientific about hunting them, you can learn all the variations and nuances and apply them appropriately. But for practical purposes, three kinds of calling will cover 90 percent of all situations — rattling, grunting, and bleating.

Whitetail bucks make scrapes as calling cards for does. Missouri hunter Jim Martin checks a small scrape for freshness. Scrapes can indicate good stand locations.

Rattling has become the most prevalent, probably because it works well, and it has gotten the most publicity, especially in Texas. But it works just as well for whitetails anywhere, as long as deer numbers are fairly high, the buck-to-doe ratio is high enough to create competition among the bucks, and bucks are engaged in pre-rut activity. The best time for rattling is during the two weeks prior to the rut, the first two weeks in November in most regions.

The grunt is one of the most common whitetail sounds. All deer make it, but it is used most by bucks during the rut, as they fight or chase does. Deer grunts are not loud, audible only up to 100 yards or so on a calm day, and have a very distinct pig-like oinking quality. Grunt calls, along with instructional tapes, have glutted the market, so you should have no trouble learning and perfecting the grunt call. Many avid whitetail hunters rely far more on the grunt call than they do on rattling (see "Calling," chapter 10).

The bleat is a sound made most commonly by does and fawns. It will attract bucks on occasion, but more often than not it attracts does. That's just as well if a buck happens to be chasing the doe that comes to your call. She'll pull him within range.

You don't read or hear much about stalking whitetails, probably because most whitetail country doesn't lend itself to stalking. But I think hunting methods are more a function of the country than the species of animal. In open terrain, you can spot and stalk whitetails just as you would mule deer in the same country. John Barsness, who lives in eastern Montana, said he frequently spots big bucks lying in weedy fencerows, coulees, and small brush patches, ideal situations for open-country stalking.

In the prairie country of South Dakota, I spotted numerous whitetails in stalkable positions in weedy draws and sparse cottonwood creek bottoms. In steep country in central Idaho and Montana, I've spotted and stalked numerous whitetails, particularly in late seasons when the deer are concentrated on lower-elevation south slopes where they're fairly easy to see.

Mule Deer

Mule deer are truly western, living from the plains states to the Pacific coast. Generally they're deer of the open country, living in alpine meadows, deserts, and prairies. They also live in dense timber in many regions, but even there they prefer the upper slopes to the creek bottoms where whitetails, which commonly occupy the same general range, spend most of their time.

A snowy background and rut activity can sometimes make bucks easy to spot in late seasons. This mule deer is on the prowl for a doe.

Pope and Young statistics show that about 70 percent of all mule deer are taken by stalking. That statistic reflects the kind of country and the time of year where most hunting takes place. Most mule deer seasons open between mid-August and early September, when two things take place that make mule deer vulnerable to stalking. First, they're still in velvet. In most regions, they'll rub off the velvet the first week in September. When mule deer are in velvet, they generally stay in fairly open country where they don't tear up their antlers on branches. They're also easy to see.

Secondly, during summer, before heavy frosts, forbs and succulent flowers and grasses thrive at high elevations above timberline and on open south and west slopes. Deer seek the most succulent foods available, so they naturally gravitate toward open country. That's one reason August finds them in high, wild, alpine country where you can spot them miles away. By mid-September, temperatures start dropping, and frost burns exposed succulents, so deer descend into timber where the forest canopy reduces the effects of frost. There, the deer are harder to see.

You've probably read that it's harder to find deer in summer than in winter, because in summer they're scattered across much broader summer range. The fact is, mule deer may be more concentrated in summer than in winter, and again, it comes back to food — and in dry country, water. They gather where the eating and drinking are easy. Commonly, on a good summer range I've spotted two to three dozen bucks a day, and up to as many as 150.

Several states hold late bow seasons following rifle seasons, starting in mid-November and running well into December. At this time, snow has forced deer from the high country onto winter ranges, where large numbers of animals are concentrated in small areas. Most winter ranges are fairly open, with only sagebrush and scattered junipers, and on a snowy background the deer are fairly easy to see. Also at this time, the bucks are in rut and are moving a lot.

Effective Hunting Methods

All of these characteristics of mule deer and their habitat make spotting and stalking a logical way to hunt.

To see lots of deer, especially during early seasons, you must get out early, right at daylight. At night, the bucks will emerge from cover and feed far into the open, and early in the morning they're still out there where they're easy to see. But by 8 or 9 A.M., when the sun starts beating down, they'll drift toward cover to bed for the day, and they'll be much tougher to see.

Whether early or late season, your most valuable hunting equipment is binoculars. Good glasses of 7x to 10x and a 20x or more powerful scope are essential for hunting mule deer (see chapter 8 for details).

Once you've spotted a buck you want, you can stalk him. (For details, see "Stalking," in chapter 10). If stalking doesn't seem feasible, you possibly can ambush a buck, a modified form of stalking. You should still spot from a distance, but watch the deer's movements to anticipate his route, and then circle around to meet him. Harold Boyack, who has bagged some of the largest bucks listed in Pope and Young, hunts this way. In the areas he hunts, deer normally bed high during the day, then move down to fields and meadows at night to feed. He starts spotting early in the morning to locate those feeding deer. He watches until they start heading uphill to their daytime bedding grounds, and then he circles ahead to cut them off. He's taken some huge bucks this way.

This type of hunting works especially well in steep mountain country, because deer normally will follow paths of least resistance. They consistently cross ridges through saddles or travel through breaks in rims. You can easily see these natural passageways and anticipate where to make your ambush.

Not all mule deer live in wide-open spaces, however. Many good mule deer areas have vast conifer forests, and others, particularly in Colorado, consist of huge aspen parks or gnarled oakbrush. Stalking isn't feasible in that type of terrain because you can't spot many deer from long range, and you can't keep them in view long enough to make a stalk.

Tree-stand hunting is the logical alternative to stalking. Several Colorado outfitters I know have given up on having their clients stalk mule deer and have resorted to tree stands instead. Their success rate varies between 30 and 50 percent, which is very high for mule deer. They place stands overlooking trails between feeding and bedding grounds, normally in aspen groves or dense fir and spruce. They scout on the ground for trails and other sign, much as they would for whitetails, but they also scout for good stand locations by spotting. Early in the morning, they spot bucks feeding in the open, and then they watch their movements toward daytime beds. From a few days of watching, they can discern the deer's patterns and anticipate where to put their stands. Many stands produce year after year.

Waterhole blinds are another method especially suited to mule deer. Some desert mule deer country is very dry, and deer are forced to come to water each day. The key word here is "dry." If water is abundant, or rain has been falling, this method can be slow. The best way to scout is simply to visit all available springs, stock tanks, and other watering spots to check for tracks. When you find one with good sign, build a ground blind or put up a tree stand if there are any suitable trees. Some of the biggest bucks, particularly in Arizona, Nevada, and southern Utah, are taken this way, but this method requires thorough scouting, and patience sitting under a blistering sun.

Black-tailed Deer

Blacktails are technically a subspecies of mule deer and have similarly branched antlers, but they are usually smaller. They often act more like whitetails, however, living in dense brush and using it to their best advantage. On the average, they're smaller in body size than whitetails and mule deer, but that doesn't mean they're tiny, as much writing would have you believe. Bucks in northern California and Oregon average 130 to 150 pounds, field-dressed, and big bucks will weigh somewhat more.

The blacktail's range extends roughly from Monterey Bay in California north through western Oregon, Washington, and British Columbia to Prince William Sound in Alaska, although those north of the Alaskan

I rattled in this blacktail during Oregon's November season. Many of the tactics that work for whitetails work for blacktails.

border are generally considered Sitka deer. Over this range, blacktails live in diverse terrain and cover. I've hunted them from the southern end of their range on the coast of Central California to northern Oregon and have come to appreciate the universal appeal and challenge of blacktails.

Central California Coast

My blacktail hunting started on the central California coast in 1977 near San Jose. I was impressed not only by the beauty of the rolling hills, with their golden fields of wild oats and dark oak groves, but also by the sheer number of deer. Season dates gave hunting there a special appeal, because along the central coast (Zone A), the bow season opens in mid-July with a two-buck limit. To my knowledge that's the earliest deer season in the country, and it gave me something to do when no other big game seasons were open.

In this region you can spot and stalk blacktails just as you would mule deer in the desert. During early and late seasons, you can spot plenty of deer out in the open wild-oat hillsides and along fringes of oak groves. Later, when the sun comes up, you have to look back into the shadowed oaks and shaded draws.

Most of the land in this region is private, and getting permission to hunt is difficult. On some ranches, you can pay to hunt; other ranches offer guided hunts. Public land—national forest, Bureau of Land Management, and state—is fairly extensive in some places, and it has some reasonably good hunting.

Blacktails have a reputation as being small, and if the reputation is deserved anywhere, it is in this region. The average buck weighs 90 to 100 pounds after field-dressing, with a big one weighing around 120 pounds. Any buck with twenty-inch antlers is a trophy, and most mature bucks have two points to the side, although some bucks grow three or four points.

Northern California

The northern California region, which extends roughly from the San Francisco Bay Area north to the Oregon border, has two major differences from Zone A to the south. One is the size of the deer. Black-tailed deer in this region aren't as big as the average mule deer, but they aren't tiny, either. Many of the big mountain blacktails of northern California weigh 150 pounds or more after field dressing, and they grow good racks. I've seen a couple over 140 (Boone and Crockett minimum is 130), and this area has produced more record-book blacktails than any other single region.

The second difference between the northern California region and Zone A is terrain and vegetation. In the foothills, you'll find oak-grasslands similar to those farther south, but you'll also find some serious mountains—up to 8,000 feet. That's especially true in the Interior Coast Range, a ridge of mountains that extends fifty miles and more inland from the coast. Above 6,000 feet, you get into semi-alpine terrain, truly a high-mountain environment. Three wilderness areas—Yolla Bolly, Trinity, and Marble Mountain—span the crest of the Interior Coast Range, and these areas have some remote country and big bucks.

Hunting here is classic mountain hunting. The canyons are steep, so you can sit on one side and spot deer moving on the other. Grassy basins and timber pockets are found at the heads of drainages and on the tops of many ridges. That's where the deer congregate, and you might see up to two or three dozen deer in these places. In fact, sheer numbers of deer can make stalking individual bucks nearly impossible, and I've often found it better to use my binoculars to locate pockets of deer, then sneak into the area in the mornings and evenings and still-hunt very slowly. The bow season in northern California runs from late August into September, and the limit in some areas is two bucks.

Oregon and Washington

California has the most record-book blacktail listings, but Oregon has most of the biggest bucks. Jackson County in southwestern Oregon has produced its share of trophy blacktails, but the Willamette Valley, a major river valley extending from Eugene north to Portland, may be the best spot for giant blacktails, particularly the Cascade foothills bordering the east side of the valley.

Many big heads, including the Boone and Crockett world record, have come from Washington. As in Oregon, the Cascade foothills, starting at the Columbia River and running north to Mount Rainier National Park, produce the biggest bucks, with the largest coming from Lewis County.

In Oregon and Washington, heavy rainfall produces forests of giant Douglas fir with an understory of ferns, blackberry brambles, and other brush too thick to walk through. Here, blacktails earn their reputation as brush-dwelling deer. In the mountain foothills, most deer live around clearcuts that have opened up the forests and allowed new plant growth. Deer feed heavily on grass and shrubs in these areas, and then bed in adjacent timber. In the valley bottoms, they hide in small woodlots and feed around the edges of cultivated fields and pastures — or in people's yards and gardens.

In some places, you can sit on log landings or ridgetops with binoculars and spot bucks feeding in clearcuts. Given the right conditions, you can stalk these blacktails. Still hunting can work, too, especially where logging has opened up the vegetation and cleared the ground for quiet footing.

But the dense vegetation lends itself more to the same methods that work for thick-cover whitetails. Tree stands are made for blacktails. Both Oregon and Washington have September archery seasons. Bucks are cautious at this time, and the best way to get a shot is to wait for them to come to you. Vegetation is so thick in some places that deer are forced to use trails. If you can find deer trails, especially intersections where two or three trails come together, you've found a good place for a blacktail stand.

The late bow seasons in Oregon and Washington, held in November and December, are probably the best times anywhere to kill truly big blacktails, because that's when the deer are rutting. Many of the same rut-hunting techniques that work for whitetails, especially antler rattling, work equally well for blacktails. From about November 10 through the end of November, blacktail bucks respond readily to rattling, and I've had excellent success rattling blacktails in Oregon at that time. You can do okay on the ground, but in the thick foliage, you'll have your best chance for getting a good shot by rattling from a tree stand.

Rub trees are good indicators of blacktail concentrations. Doug Chase looks over a cedar tree that lost a fight with a blacktail buck.

13

Elk, Black Bears, and Antelope

Next to deer, the most popular game animals among archers are elk, black bears, and antelope. Each has its own special challenges, and they're all great archery animals.

Elk

The best elk states—Washington, Oregon, Idaho, Montana, Wyoming, Colorado, New Mexico, Arizona, and Utah—all have bow seasons during the rut, and hunting elk by calling is the best all-around method for bowhunting. For best results, you need to learn two types of calls: bugling, the sound made by rutting bulls; and cow calling (or herd talk). I can't describe these in print, but dozens of companies make audio and video tapes on elk calling, so you'll have no trouble finding good material.

For bugling, the choice of calls is endless—whistles, reed calls, diaphragms—with many variations on each. Cow sounds can be made with any of the diaphragm calls, but the most common cow calls are made with rubber bands that squeal as you blow across them. My personal choice for all calling is the mouth diaphragm, but those don't work for everyone. Experiment until you find the right style for you.

Elk are herd animals that live in pockets, and you must understand their habits to find them. The key to finding them during the rut—late

Most western states have bow seasons during the elk rut. Bulls are easier to fool, especially by calling, when they're preoccupied with cows.

August through the first week in October—is water, especially in the form of springs, seeps, wet meadows, and similar damp spots. They like the coolness of these locations, and they use the mud for wallows.

Elk don't like heat, so they require cool shade during the day. They like thick brush and cover as protection from predators. Most good elk country has stands of dark spruce or fir timber, thick brush, tangled piñon pine and juniper, or similar dense cover.

Elk are grazers by preference, so you'll find them around grassy meadows, the same kind of feed that would attract cattle. However, some good elk country has very little grass. If that's the case, elk will browse on shrubs such as alder, willow, and huckleberries.

With some thoughtful looking, you can predict the location of places with the required water, cover, and food before setting foot on the ground. Large-scale topographic maps show minute detail, including most springs, so search out every spring on your map, and consider them as starting points. In particular, look for bowls or basins. Snow forms in cornices around the rims of north- or east-facing bowls. Come spring, it soaks into the ground and forms an underground reservoir, which leaks out into the floor of the bowls all summer.

These guidelines will get you into good places. Then, as you investigate likely pockets, judge the sign, especially a concentration of fresh tracks and deeply cut trails. In core areas, you should find lots of droppings, and you'll find fresh beds and urine spots. You may also notice a rich barnyard smell. You should find fresh rub trees and wallows, as well.

Using a bugle or a cow call is one of the best ways to locate and attract elk.

When you get into such a place, use all your senses. You may see or smell animals, but you're most likely to hear them first. Elk are vocal, so use your calls to talk to them. Don't wait until you hear a bull to begin calling; blow your call to make him respond. You might start by bugling. That will often get a response from an aggressive bull. If that doesn't work, try cow calling. Mix up your calling, trying a little of that, until you hit on something that works.

Sooner or later, if you continue calling in good country, you'll get a response. It might be a full-blown bugle, or it might just be a low grunt or chuckle. It doesn't matter how the elk responds. The fact that you now know his location is the important point.

To call the bull to you, try to get within 200 yards or so, always keeping the wind in your favor, and then find a good place to hide and start calling. I usually start by bugling, and sometimes that's all that's needed. Some bulls will come on the run. If bugling doesn't work, switch to cow calling, or try a combination of both. Or quit calling altogether and simply rake a tree with a branch to sound like a bull rubbing his antlers on a tree.

Once you have a bull coming your way, wait until he presents a close, open shot. At long ranges in timber, you simply can't gauge all branches and twigs between you and an animal, and arrow deflections are common. That's why you want close shots. A good shot on elk is somewhere between ten and twenty yards. In most cases, I would consider thirty yards a long shot on elk. Also, wait for a broadside shot. Elk are tough, and a bad hit means a wounded and lost animal. Good shot placement is critical in elk hunting.

Still hunting can be deadly under the right conditions, and many hunters take big bulls by hunting from tree stands overlooking well-used trails or wallows. But calling is the primary method used by most hunters during the rut.

Black Bears

Black bears are the most widely distributed game animals in North America, which puts them within reach of many hunters. Only the heavily farmed midwestern states are without black bears. In some areas with spring seasons, they can be hunted at times when no other big game seasons are open. A bear rug or shoulder mount makes an excellent trophy, and black bears are good eating, although I doubt many hunters shoot bears just for the meat. These are some of the reasons for the growing popularity of hunting black bears.

Black bears have a wide distribution in North America. Bear hunting has become a strong tradition among archers.

Regulations for bear hunting are varied. Some states have spring seasons, others don't. Some states allow baiting or hunting with hounds, some don't. This section includes a few general principles about bear hunting. Check local regulations before you go hunting to see which restrictions apply.

Baiting

Pope and Young data show that nearly 70 percent of all black bears entered in the record book are taken by baiting. Baiting bears has become one of the strongest bowhunting traditions, and some archers would no more miss their annual bait hunt for bears than they'd miss scrape hunting for whitetails or bugling for elk.

Some people question the sporting aspect of baiting, but planning a bait hunt takes time, energy, and money. Collecting, storing, and distributing huge quantities of bait can be an onerous task. In regions where the country is flat and dense, baiting is about the only feasible way to hunt bears.

The idea behind baiting is to create a food source that will hold bears in one small area and pull them into view for a shot. To do that, you have to feed them well. Many hunters stock 500 pounds or more of bait at several stations every week.

Meat scraps bought from slaughter houses for a reasonable price are the most common bait, but other foods work as well. Some hunters collect used cooking grease from restaurants, and others get beaver carcasses from trappers. In the fall, when bears are putting on fat, apples and other fruits work well, but probably the favorite bait of all is pastries — sweet rolls and donuts. These are fairly easy to acquire from stores and bakeries, and bears love them.

Rotting meat or other strong foods — canned sardines or anise oil, for example — also have value, because their smell attracts bears from long distances. Bait stations should be placed in dense brush, where the bears will feel comfortable feeding during daylight hours. They should also be away from roads where other hunters can't find them, especially hound hunters, who may run bears that are hitting your baits.

Most hunters use tree stands over bait. Shots from stands should be made at no more than ten to twenty yards from the target. Bears have amazingly sensitive noses, so stands should always be placed downwind of bait. Their ears are nearly as good as their noses, so a stand must be absolutely silent. Even the slightest squeak will send a bear running, as will the sound of an arrow sliding across a rest. At ten yards, a bear will hear those sounds instantly, and he won't wait around.

Try to arrange the bait so a bear must present a good shot, broadside or quartering slightly away. If you just pile bait in an opening, bears can eat facing any direction. By placing the bait against or between rocks or trees, you can lead bears to good positions for shots. You also can direct bears by cutting holes on only one side of a barrel or by making a log crib like the corner of a split-rail fence to force a bear to stand at a particular angle to eat.

Arrow-hit bears often leave poor blood trails because their fat tends to seal the arrow hole and their long fur absorbs much blood. Be sure that your shooting angle will result in a double-lung hit, and consider using a string tracker. This device, which screws into the stabilizer hole on a bow, contains a spool of fine thread. The end of this thread is attached to your hunting arrow, and when the arrow hits an animal, thread is pulled from the spool, leaving an easy-to-follow trail of thread. The string affects arrow flight very little out to twenty yards, and the tracker can help you recover hard-to-find bears.

Hound Hunting

Hunting with hounds is the second-most-common method for taking bears. Houndmen drive along back roads, watching for bear tracks. A good bear hunter can spot the flattened depression of a bear track instantly on the shoulder or bank of a road. When a fresh track is located, the hounds are released to run the bear.

Many houndmen also locate bears with strike dogs, hounds with especially sharp noses. The strike dog is tethered on a box in the back of a pickup truck (or on the hood). The hunter drives slowly along back roads. When the strike dog smells a bear, he starts barking, and the hounds are released to run the bear.

In good bear country, hound hunting is a fairly sure method, but it's not easy. Bears will lead hounds into the roughest country, and they can go for miles. You have to be in good shape, but if you're short on time, hiring a guide who uses hounds is probably the quickest and surest way to collect a black bear.

Spotting and Stalking

If your only goal is to kill a bear, hunt with bait or dogs. But if you like a challenge, try hunting bears strictly with your eyes and on foot. I've taken a couple this way and have had many other exciting close calls. This method is especially adapted to the West, where steep mountains and relatively open country make spotting easier.

To spot bears, you have to know their food sources. In spring, bears just coming out of hibernation graze in the open, where they're relatively easy to see. Any meadow, clearcut, or other opening with tender, green grass will attract spring bears. Wild onions are common spring foods in parts of the West. Bears will also devour carrion, so winter ranges where deer and elk have died are especially good places to hunt. The middle two weeks in May may be the best time to hunt in the spring, but hunting can be good from mid-April through June.

Early fall offers excellent spotting, too. As always, bears will congregate around food sources—berries, fruit (in abandoned orchards), and acorns or other mast. To improve your chances of spotting bears, learn the main sources in your hunting area at any given time of year.

As in any game spotting, good binoculars are essential. A bear in the open is fairly easy to see, but you may need a scope to judge size and fur quality.

The secret to spotting bears is patience. Relative scarcity alone makes them hard to see. The fact that they're generally solitary (except sows with cubs) compounds the problem. A single animal is always harder to spot than a herd. Therefore, the best approach is to pick out some likely country and to sit there and watch it for a long time, at least a couple of hours. In mixed brush and openings, a bear may be hidden at first, but if you watch long enough, he'll eventually move into view. If you just look for five minutes and move on, you'll overlook a lot of bears. Early and late in the day are best, but I've spotted plenty of bears at midday, too. Don't give up too early.

Stalking within bow range of bears is no cinch. They have relatively poor eyesight, so that's your major advantage. But what they lack in sight, they make up for with their senses of smell and hearing. Follow the steps outlined under "Stalking" in chapter 10, and pay particular attention to

I took this desert antelope while hunting from a pit blind near a spring.

ways to avoid being smelled and heard. With some time and effort, you can sneak within good bow range of a bear.

Antelope

Antelope are numerous and are hunted in all eleven western states except Washington. They're also heavily hunted in the Dakotas and Nebraska. Antelope can be difficult or easy to bag, depending on how you hunt them. Although they might seem impossible to approach, because of their fantastic eyesight and the wide-open country they inhabit, hunting statistics show that bowhunters can kill antelope. In 1989 in Colorado, archers had a 30-percent success rate; in Wyoming it was 40 percent. That's good hunting success no matter how you hunt.

Waterhole Blinds

The antelope's major weakness is the need to water every day, especially in August and September when most archery seasons are held. Pope and Young data show that nearly 60 percent of all antelope were taken from blinds, and undoubtedly most of those were waterhole blinds. If water is

Waterhole blinds offer the surest way to take antelope. Scout waterholes by looking for tracks and by using high-power optics to watch herd movements.

abundant in springs and creeks, or heavy rains have fallen, you can't rely on antelope coming to specific waterholes. But in typical prairie and desert antelope country, water is limited to springs or stock tanks, and antelope must come to these places sooner or later.

You can scout by checking for tracks around waterholes, but don't limit your scouting to that. Antelope are so visible, you can scout best with your eyes. For scouting, 8x or 10x binoculars are a minimum, and a scope of at least 20x helps more. Watch potential waterholes for a few days, and you'll get a good idea of what to expect there.

If possible, build blinds on two or three waterholes to give yourself some options, particularly in relation to wind direction. Several times antelope have smelled me and approached my blind, but in such cases they've been tense and ready to bolt. They'll be much more relaxed and less likely to jump the string if they never smell you, so place stands downwind of waterholes. And, if at all possible, keep the sun behind you so the antelope must look into the sun to see you.

Ninety percent of the success of an antelope hunt depends on the blind. With a good blind, you've got 'em; with a poor blind, you don't. On my first antelope hunt, I discovered antelope watering at a little seeping spring on a desert flat, so I scratched out a shallow blind in the sagebrush and started my vigil. Just after sunrise I spotted a fine antelope buck two miles away. He walked steadily toward me until he stood twenty-five yards away. By the time he got there, I was tighter than a fiddle string. When his head went down to drink, I slowly raised my bow, but before I could draw, the antelope was leaving a dust cloud one hundred yards away.

With 270-degree, 10x vision, antelope miss nothing; even the slight hint of a bow tip above the sagebrush will catch their eye. You must be able to shoot without visible movement, which means digging a deep and roomy pit. If you're scrunched up in a little hole, you'll never get a shot. Use a shovel and a pick to dig a deep pit. Include a built-in seat so you can sit up comfortably without being seen and shoot without moving — except to draw your bow. Practice shooting from the blind to make sure you've got plenty of clearance for your bow tips.

The next step is to conceal the pit. In sagebrush or grasslands, you'll have cover to work with. To build a good blind, you need four 2 x 2 stakes and fifteen to twenty feet of two-foot chicken wire. Drive stakes at each corner of the pit and tie the chicken wire around three sides. Also make a wire top over the blind. Shade from the top will hide you and help keep you cool during long summer days in the blind.

Once you've built the framework, gather grass and brush to cover the top and sides (an ax or saw is handy for cutting sagebrush). Don't be skimpy, especially in the back. Your blind should have a solid backdrop to eliminate your silhouette. Leave some peepholes in the sides so you can see without sticking your head out.

With a good blind, you're 90 percent of the way to an antelope. The only other ingredient is time. Most hunters agree you must be in your blind before daylight and that mid-morning is the most likely time to get a shot. Pope and Young statistics show that about 65 percent of all antelope are killed between sunrise and 2 P.M. Don't be in a hurry to leave, though. Several successful hunters have told me they've had some of the best bucks come in right at sundown.

Stalking

The second most effective method for taking antelope, at about 30 percent according to Pope and Young statistics, is stalking. Antelope lend themselves to stalking because they're highly visible, but the country must be right. In table-flat, knee-high grass, you can just about forget it. But a lot of good antelope country is broken with many draws, ravines, and hills, and some of it has high sage and junipers that offer good cover. With some decent cover, you have at least a reasonable chance of stalking a buck. Your chances of stalking within bow range of a herd aren't good, however. Lone bucks are far easier.

To plan a stalk, find a good vantage point at first light and use your binoculars and scope to locate a buck. Antelope often will walk a fairly straight course, particularly heading to water, and sometimes you can ambush them. In other cases, you may do better to wait for them to bed. After going to water and feeding, antelope often lie down by 9 or 10 A.M. After one buck lay in the shade of a juniper, I lined up with the tree he was lying behind so he couldn't see me and walked within thirty yards of him. Then I missed him. (See chapter 10 for more details on stalking.)

Decoying

Decoying is to antelope what calling is to elk and deer, because it's a method of pulling antelope to you. You can make an antelope silhouette decoy out of plywood and either paint it or cover it with scraps of rug. You also can buy commercial decoys, most of which are made of molded plastic and are fairly lightweight.

The best time to decoy antelope is from the last week in August until about September 15, the time when bucks are establishing their rutting territories. At this time they will aggressively chase other bucks (or decoys that look like bucks) to run them off—that's why decoys work well then.

To use a decoy, you first must spot a buck at long range. Then, using terrain to stay hidden, crawl within 200 yards or so of the buck and very slowly raise and set up your decoy (it should have a stake that you can push into the ground). Often, when a buck sees this intruder he'll come on the run, so you have to be ready to shoot quickly. Most serious decoy hunters wait until the buck comes within range and then rise to shoot over the top of the decoy.

Several states have archery antelope seasons during early September, the ideal time for decoying, but some hold rifle seasons then. It should go without saying, but I'll emphasize the point here—don't use a decoy during the firearms season.

14

A Parting Shot

The preceding pages have, I hope, given you fundamentals that will launch you into a long, successful, and enjoyable bowhunting career. You will succeed as a bowhunter if you master these basics and then advance beyond them, through reading, videos, exposure to successful bowhunters, and, perhaps most of all, personal experience. More that that, I hope you learn simply to enjoy the sport. Shooting a bow is fun, something you can do year-round, even in your own backyard or basement. And hunting with a bow, because of its very nature, can be rewarding and memorable.

Bowhunting is a sport unto itself, not just glorified rifle hunting. Rifle hunters don't become bowhunters just by changing weapons. Becoming a bowhunter requires a change of attitude. Statistics from Idaho help paint the picture. In 1988, rifle deer hunters had a 49-percent success rate and hunted eleven days for each deer taken, compared to bowhunters' 16-percent success rate and forty-six days per deer taken. That means bowhunters had a success rate less than one-third the rate for rifle hunters, and they spent more than four times as long in the field for each deer taken. The specifics vary slightly among states, but the trend holds everywhere, and it makes one point clear — for success as a bowhunter, you simply have to hunt longer and harder than rifle hunters do. Bowhunting is a game of patience and dedication. To be a bowhunter, you have to love hunting for the sake of hunting. If killing animals is your only goal, you should try other methods.

Because of the time required and the relative difficulty of getting good shots, bowhunting demands confidence. In fact, I would rate confidence as one of the major, if not *the* major, ingredient for being a good bowhunter. Confidence is self-fulfilling — if you think you can do it, you'll find ways to make it happen. A study on world-class archers showed that one major variable in tournament success was confidence. The very best archers had a high degree of confidence without worrying about past mistakes.

Confidence starts with the very basis for this book — fundamentals. Choose your tackle thoughtfully and tune it well so you know it will perform. Then work on perfecting your shooting ability and learning basic hunting skills so you know you can perform. Your confidence will grow as you gain experience in the field.

Many experienced bowhunters have told me they think beginners should shoot the first deer they get a good shot at, because you learn by doing. If you wait forever for the biggie, you will never get the experience you need to take him when you get the chance. This happened to me early in my hunting career. I had visions of killing a giant desert mule deer, so that's what I tried for. I could fill a book with stories of my botched attempts at good bucks. Then one day, I saw a spike buck lying under a tree, and, to make a long story short, I got him. I can't report that my bowhunting career instantly became one constant string of successes, but that first buck changed my whole attitude. It showed me that I could do it, and my confidence grew. Yours will, too. With any success, no matter how small, you'll build a reservoir of experience, and confidence will evolve until you won't question whether you'll get an animal; you'll know you will.

When I first hunted with Larry D. Jones, a well-known elk-call maker, the thing that impressed me most was not that Larry did everything perfectly and killed every bull elk he went after, but his ability to accept failure and to keep hunting hard. When we tried calling in one bull and it didn't work, Larry was ready to get on to the next one. That's why he's known for success. It's not because he never fouls up; it's because he never gives up. With a bow, you can't expect to get within range of every animal or to make a perfect shot every time. More often than not, things will go wrong. Good bowhunters are not discouraged by that fact. They just keep trying.

A common bowhunting joke used to be that you got animals by shooting all your arrows into the air and then going out to see if any of them hit anything. Unfortunately, that idea may have more truth than some of us would like to admit. Years ago, archers relied on arrow power

If you play the game well and fairly, you'll find bowhunting the greatest sport of all.

more than accuracy to take animals. It was a lot of fun launching arrows into the air, hoping you'd eventually connect.

Gradually, with improvements in tackle and shooting knowledge, the many-arrows approach is giving way to a one-shot, one-kill philosophy. I think that's good. One major black eye for bowhunting is wounding loss. The problem isn't nearly as great as some people make it out to be, but one animal needlessly wounded and lost is too many. For the sake of the animals, for our own peace of mind and satisfaction at a job well done, and for the future of bowhunting, our goal should be zero wounding loss. That's attainable, but it requires restraint in shot selection as well as dedication to equipment and practice. We need a reversal of attitude from the old days, a change from the idea that "I can't get something unless I put some arrows in the air" to the philosophy that "I won't put an arrow in the air until I know I can get something."

In recent years, many bowhunters have placed great emphasis on killing trophy animals and entering them in the record books. That's not bad in itself because it provides higher goals and added challenge, which can make us work harder and become better hunters. Unfortunately, the drive to excel has led some people do almost anything to kill more and bigger animals. Several hunters, famous for their big bucks or bulls, have been discredited, either through game-law convictions or for using unethical means to enter animals into the record books, and a number have had their animals thrown out of the Pope and Young record book for those reasons. Breaking the rules to look good is like winning a card game by changing the rules as you play. The only victory in hunting or any other pursuit is winning under established rules. Learn to play the bowhunting game fairly, and you'll enjoy the greatest pursuit of all.

Index